The Virtuous Fall of the Girls from Our Lady of Sorrows

by Gina Femia

The Virtuous Fall of the Girls From Our Lady of Sorrows was developed and produced through The Writer-in-Residence Program at Spicy Witch Productions *(Rebecca Weiss, Artistic Director, Phoebe Brooks, Programming Director, Hannah Hammel, Marketing & PR Director, Isabelle Russo, Development Director)* and received its World Premiere at The Flea Theater May 2019.

The original cast was as follows:
MIA CANTER - Sister Ignatius and others
SHAVANA CLARKE - Dove
ALIA GUIDRY - Imogene
ASHIL LEE - Maxx
RENITA LEWIS - Minnie
SARAH ROSENGARTEN - Jenny
PEARL SHIN - Mathilda

The original creative team was as follows:
BLAYZE TEICHER - Director
YI-CHUNG CHEN - Lighting Design
LINDSAY GENEVIEVE FUORI - Scenic Design
CARSEN JOENK - Sound Design
MEGAN MCQUEENEY - Props Design
NOELLE QUANCI - Costume Design
FRANCES SWANSON - Production Stage Manager

ALL RIGHTS RESERVED
Original Works Publishing

CAUTION: Professionals and amateurs are hereby warned that this play is subject to royalty. It is fully protected by Original Works Publishing and the copyright laws of the United States. All rights, including professional, amateur, motion pictures, recitation, lecturing, public reading, radio broadcasting, television, and the rights of translation into foreign languages are strictly reserved.

The performance rights to this play are controlled by Original Works Publishing and royalty arrangements and licenses must be secured well in advance of presentation. No changes of any kind shall be made to the work, including without limitation any changes to characterization, intent, time, place, gender or race of the character. PLEASE NOTE that amateur royalty fees are set upon application in accordance with your producing circumstances. When applying for a royalty quotation and license please give us the number of performances intended, dates of production, your seating capacity and admission fee. Royalty of the required amount must be paid whether the play is presented for charity or gain and whether or not admission is charged. Royalties are payable with negotiation from Original Works Publishing.

Due authorship credit must be given anywhere the title appears, on all programs, printing and advertising for the play. The name of the Playwright must appear on a separate line, in which no other name appears, immediately beneath the title and in size and prominence of type equal to 50% of the largest, most prominent letter used for the title of the Work. No person, firm or entity may receive credit larger or more prominent than that accorded to the Playwright.

Copying from this book in whole or in part is strictly forbidden by law, and the right of performance is not transferable. The purchase of this publication does not constitute a license to perform the work.

Whenever the play is produced, the following notice must appear on all programs, printing, and advertising for the play on separate line:
"Produced by special arrangement with
Original Works Publishing.
www.originalworksonline.com"

THE VIRTUOUS FALL OF THE GIRLS
FROM OUR LADY OF SORROWS
© Gina Femia
Trade Edition, 2025
ISBN 978-1-63092-146-0

Also Available From Gina Femia

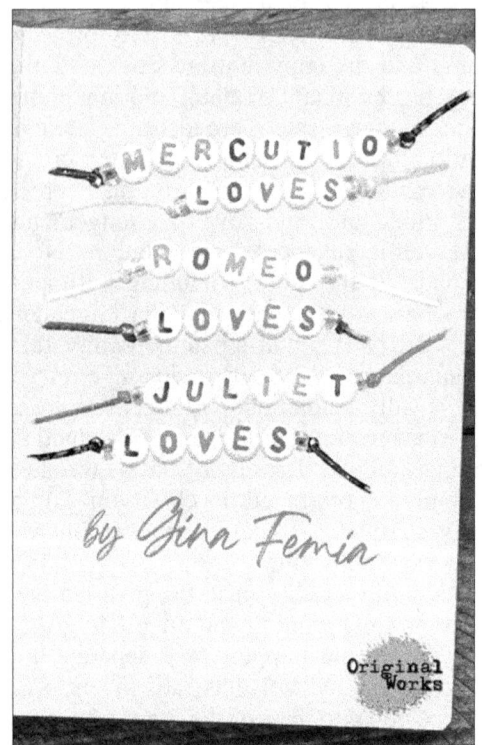

MERCUTIO LOVES ROMEO LOVES JULIET LOVES

Synopsis: Ellie and Britt have been lifelong friends, lifelong haters of cheerleaders and lifelong drama geeks, so when their All Girls Catholic School's drama club does Romeo and Juliet, obviously they'll be a part of it. But when Amber, a cheerleader with an injury unexpectedly gets the lead across from Britt, Ellie's heart is turned upside down. Actually, all their hearts are.
Cast Size: 2 Females, 1 ENBY

Folks:

Minnie: A senior, our scribe. Her personality is so big, wondrous and bubbly, it's hard for people to take her seriously sometimes – but they totally should, 18.

Imogene: A senior, Minnie's best friend. Androgynous, rough talking, tough but has an incredible ability to be vulnerable, 18.

Jenny: A junior, super feminine to the max, wants to be a movie star when she grows up, 17.

Mathilda: A freshman, she's always aiming to please, naïve but honest and truthful and incredibly authentic, 14.

Dove: A sophomore, Minnie's younger sister, literally only doing this because her parents told her to do it, wears her hurt on her heart, 15.

Maxx: A sophomore, has been sentenced to drama club as part of her delinquency and punishment and all that, glares at the world, 15.

One actor plays the following roles:

Sister Ignatius: Teaches religion and morality, she is also Minnie's advisor and second in command of the school. Stern. Unflinching in her belief, still wears a habit, 30.
Sister Rose: Teaches History, a little show-boaty.
Sister Lucy: Teaches Chemistry, crotchety and old.
Mrs. O'Donell: Teaches a workshop on menstruation, bubbly and warm.

All these characters have been defined as 'girls' or 'women' by society, but a person of any gender, who is comfortable playing a 'girl' may inhabit these roles.

Setting:

Our Lady of Sorrows, a rundown all-girl's catholic high school out in East NY, Brooklyn that's been part of the neighborhood for over 70 years.

Most of the play takes place in the Gym/Theatre hybrid but there are scenes that take place in other parts of the school like the library, cafeteria, a classroom and a bathroom, too.

A blank space with a prop and sound will work more efficiently than built sets.

Time:

September – November, 2002.

Playwrights' Note:
When sentences end without punctuation, there is something unfinished about them. The next sentence does not cut off the first, but comes quickly after.

THE VIRTUOUS FALL OF THE GIRLS
FROM OUR LADY OF SORROWS

PROLOGUE

(We begin, as the world did; in darkness.
But not silence.
Like, it would be pretty sick if something like Nas' The Cross can play in that darkness until suddenly The Stage Manager is like Let There Be Light! and the music cuts out as warm lights rise on SISTER IGNATIUS.
She stands at a podium, arms open in greeting.)

SISTER IGNATIUS: and I am happy to share that your voices have been heard and Taco Tuesdays will be reinstated throughout the entirety of the 2002-2003 school year.
(Maybe she does a little fist pump like thing to punctuate that she is excited! for! them!)
Now girls. I know that coming back from summer vacation and getting back into School Mode isn't easy. I hope you spent the summer months unproductive and worry free because that means you're coming back fresh, refreshed, and ready to tackle the year!
Here at Our Lady of Sorrows, we want you to grow into the woman that God intends for you to be. He has great plans for you, plans so big and so large, you can't even see them yet.
You know, it is true that God works in mysterious ways, there are little signs from Him scattered about our days, even in the most mundane cracks of our lives.
Just the other day, I was in a Rite Aid, wandering aimlessly down the aisles when a decorative plaque caught my eye. I don't why it did, I have no need for a decorative plaque, but I noticed it had a saying, and it actually made me think of all of you.
(She takes out a piece of paper and reads from it.)
'Shoot for the moon.
And even if you fall,
you'll land among the stars.'
(She is so pleased with herself.)
So welcome, ladies!

On behalf of Sister Anne and myself, welcome to another year of growth, reflection and –

(Lights go out suddenly and a spotlight shakily finds its way to MINNIE, in a completely different part of the auditorium; she has appeared from outta nowhere. She's wearing something like a monk's robe and a half mask or something that kinda hides who she is. She speaks with all the drama her heart can muster:)

MINNIE: Lust.
   Sex.
   Lies.
   MURDER.
   All of these things?
   are Sins,
   the things we know are Wrong in the eyes of our Lord *(crosses herself)*,
   but they are the things that compose our human souls!
   Which is why
   when these things are all mixed together,
   they are the perfect ingredients to make a play.
   And speaking of plays,
   (she turns more into a show-person)
   Auditions for M4M2, a new play by yours truly (adaptedfromthetextofwilliamshakespeare) are gonna be held today, after school at –

SISTER INGATIUS: Minerva Green!

(The scene shifts suddenly from the auditorium to Sister Ignatius' office.)

MINNIE: Come on, Sister, it's not that serious –

SISTER IGNATIUS: It wasn't the time

MINNIE: I was just embracing my greatness,

SISTER IGNATIUS: or the place to -

MINNIE: shooting for the moon…

SISTER IGNATIUS: Don't

MINNIE: …falling among the stars…

SISTER IGNATIUS: It's not a joke

MINNIE: Who's joking, I'm being serious, dead serious – what, you've never heard of a Dramatic Opening?

SISTER IGNATIUS: You can't just interrupt an assembly in the name of Drama!

MINNIE: I had to do SOMETHING, Sister Anne told me I couldn't do an announcement, but auditions are TODAY-

SISTER IGNATIUS: And you should've listened

MINNIE: Okay, sure, but how're people supposed to know about it if they don't hear about it?! She's trying to sabotage me, Sister Ignatius, I swear –

SISTER IGNATIUS: Don't swear

MINNIE: Fine, I Mean It Seriously, Sister Anne's been trying to sabotage me since the start!

SISTER IGNATIUS: Well Sister Anne is reconsidering –

MINNIE: What, no!

SISTER IGNATIUS: and I can't say I don't agree -

MINNIE: I was just JOKING! It was just a JOKE

SISTER IGNATIUS: Have you ever seen Sister Anne crack a smile let alone laugh?
At a JOKE?

MINNIE: But it's my senior thesis!

SISTER IGNATIUS: You'll write a paper like everyone else

MINNIE: But I don't wanna be like everyone else

SISTER IGNATIUS: There's nothing wrong with being like everyone else

MINNIE: How am I supposed to be great and like shooting for the moon when I'm also supposed to be like everyone else?!

SISTER IGNATIUS: I've been on your side since the beginning, I think it's a good idea, it is a good idea, but Sister Anne didn't trust it "Where is the value?" she wanted to know "Where is the LEARNING POTENTIAL" because she didn't see it but I could and so who convinced her?

MINNIE: You.

SISTER IGNATIUS: Yes, me, I did,

MINNIE: I know

SISTER IGNATIUS: I did that for you because I believed in you!
And maybe that was my mistake.

(Minnie feels bad in spite of herself.)

SISTER IGNATIUS: It's time for class.

(Sister Ignatius gestures to the door. Minnie stands. Turns to leave. But turns back to Sister Ignatius instead.)

MINNIE: I'm sorry.
  Seriously, Sister, I'm sorry.
  I wasn't thinking.
  I think.
  I was just thinking about my dad and.
  I dunno, I wasn't thinking.

(there's a beat)

MINNIE: But. Can you please –
  I don't wanna not do it just because I fuc-messed up.
  I already wrote it and
  the thing with plays is that they're meant to be alive, you know?

Like, not just stuck on pages like novels and shi-stuff.
They're supposed to be alive, to live in the world, out loud.

SISTER IGNATIUS: If everybody in the world who ever wrote a play had their plays "come to life", we'd run out of time in the world.
My nephew's written a play.
Our mailman's written a play.
The woman in the coffee cart on Myrtle avenue's written a play.

MINNIE: Yeah, but I wrote this one. *(beat)* Please?

(A beat where Sister Ignatius considers.)

SISTER IGNATIUS: I'll talk to Sister Anne. See what I can do.

(Minnie runs over and hugs Sister Ignatius. Sister Ignatius starts to hug her but stops herself.)

SISTER IGNATIUS: You better not let me down, Minnie. I believe in you.

MINNIE: Yeah, I believe in me, too.

SISTER IGNATIUS: I'm being serious -

MINNIE: So am I –
I won't let you down.
Swear -
I mean, I Mean It Seriously –

SISTER INGATIUS: You can just promise.

MINNIE: Yeah, okay, that works. I promise. I won't let you down.

(Music starts blasting as the lights shift – a vignette scored by music – instrumental and funky, it leads us into -)

MOVEMENT I

(We hear an aggressive school bell, remixed into the music and the girls mill through the hall – it should feel fuller than it actually is.

We see JENNY *and* IMOGENE *walking down the hall, playing a couple of handheld videogames side by side while* MAXX *walks by and picks a lip gloss out of Jenny's pocket*

MATHILDA *is lost, frantically looking at her schedule and the sea of doors whose numbers don't match what is in the hall.*

Sister Ignatius walks past a crucifix and crosses herself while she does so.

Mathilda reaches out to her for help but she continues down the hall, not noticing her.

Maxx realizes she pick-pocketed lip gloss from Jenny which is lame, so she puts it back in Jenny's pocket as Jenny reaches to put it on, laughing at something Imogene said.

Dove walks by Mathilda, who mimes asking her for directions, but she ignores her,

rolls up on Minnie, her sister, who ignores her.

Minnie puts up a poster, something that says Auditions for new play M4M2 happening today!

Students gather around it to look at different intervals.

Mathilda still doesn't know where she's going.

at the height of it all, everybody who's gotta winds up on the stage in the gym and we begin -)

SCENE I

(There are chairs on the stage but the girls sit around them rather than in them. Jenny, Imogene, and Dove are the only ones there.

Dove is lying on the stage, listening to her discman with her eyes closed.
Maybe we can hear the super angsty music she's listening to.
Imogene and Jenny are in the middle of an important conversation.)

JENNY: Nah

IMOGENE: Deadass

JENNY: You're LYING!

IMOGENE: I'm not!

JENNY: Prove it

IMOGENE: Prove it how, I just told you –

JENNY: PROVE it –

IMOGENE: Everybody knows it!

JENNY: Nobody knows shit, you're lying, Imogene

IMOGENE: am not

JENNY: just like the time you told me I could get herpes from a toilet seat

IMOGENE: yo, you CAN get herpes from a toilet seat!

JENNY: Yeah well my aunt's a nurse and she told me you CAN'T.

IMOGENE: how'd my cousin get herpes then?!

JENNY: I dunno, probably by blowing a buncha dirty-dick guys?

IMOGENE: That's not the only way you get it

JENNY: That's not what my aunt says -

IMOGENE: I bet your aunt would know this, you've got a cell phone, let's call her right now

JENNY: You kidding, I'm not wasting my minutes on this shit, this made up nonsense shit, besides, if it IS such common fuckin' knowledge then any everyday random joe would know it, so like all you need to do is just literally ask somebody – anybody – and have Them know in order to prove your weak ass point.

IMOGENE: Ask who, there's nobody here! This place is like a morgue right now, shit.

(Dove kinda hears this and tries to subtly shift into a more hidden position, away from them.)

IMOGENE: Yo, Sparrow! Sparrow! *(to Jenny)* What's her name?

(Jenny shrugs.)

IMOGENE: She's Minnie's sister

JENNY: So? Do I look like, a historian, like I should know Minnie's entire family tree?

IMOGENE: SPARROW. SPARROW.

(Dove finally looks up.)

DOVE: My name's not Sparrow.

IMOGENE: It's got something to do with birds –

DOVE: Yeah, Dove

JENNY: Like the chocolate?

DOVE: No, like the bird

JENNY: Oh, yeah

IMOGENE: Tell Jenny that dogs get periods

DOVE: Ew, what they do?

JENNY: See? I told ya - Nobody knows that shit.

IMOGENE: How do you think baby animals happen?

(Mathilda enters. She's very skittish. Nobody says hi to her and she doesn't really know how to say hi to people so she kinda just awkwardly walks onto the stage and slinks into one of the chairs.)

JENNY: I dunno! All our dogs are spayed

DOVE: Mine, too

JENNY: So they literally can't make babies

DOVE: Mine either

MATHILDA: My dog's name is Peppermint.

(There's an awkward moment where they look at Mathilda. She is unphased.)

MATHILDA: She's a Maltese.

(Awkward beat. They ignore her.)

JENNY: So what happens then, they just walk around with blood all pouring outta them?

DOVE: They make doggie tampons?

IMOGENE: No, doggie diapers, to catch it, but sometimes the dogs wiggle outta them and then we come home and there's blood all smeared on the floor

(all the girls ew and make sounds that are like Holy shit, that's so gross!)

IMOGENE: It's not that serious!

JENNY: It sounds kinda serious!

IMOGENE: No I mean, it's not as much as like when humans get it or anything, and it doesn't happen to them as much, only like once every six months but it happens in dogs and it happens in all mammals and that's how babies are born.

MATHILDA: It's like the circle of life!

(They all stare at her.)

MATHILDA: You know because like….Reproduction.

IMOGENE: Who the fuck are you again?

MATHILDA: Oh, hi, I'm Mathilda

(She kinda half stands with her hand out to shake but realizes that people in high school don't shake hands so like kinda sits but not really with her hand out, it's madd awkward.)

JENNY: You a freshman?

MATHILDA: Kinda!

DOVE: How are you kind've a freshman

MATHILDA: I mean, I am!
   That is what I am.
   I'm fresh.

(She is pleased with her joke. nobody else gets it.)

DOVE: Okay.

(They lapse into a semi-awkward silence.)

JENNY: I wish I only got my period every six months.
   I've got cramps so bad it feels like my insides are trying to crawl out my ass.

IMOGENE: You need a Tylenol?

JENNY: You got?

IMOGENE: Yeah

JENNY: Yeah, can I get some – Nurse Cathy cut me off

IMOGENE: What a bitch

JENNY: I know, I went at third period and she gave me two and I took'em and I felt better but then it like wore off around sixth period, right after lunch, and I swear they hurt so bad, I couldn't breathe – like, I could literally barely breathe, they hurt so bad – and I asked her for two more and she crossed her arms and she was like "Jenny, you know this is medicine, not candy, right?"

DOVE: Ew.

JENNY: I know, and then she like took my hand and was like Jenny, why don't you tell me what's REALLY bothering you, like I was trying to avoid a math test or something but I was like Nurse Cathy it is literally the third day of school, I don't have ANYthing to do, can you just give me a fucking Tylenol so I can go about my day not wanting to die and she just sent me back to class, wouldn't even let me use the heating pad, shit, it's not like it's my fault my period decided to coincide with the first week of school.

(A beat as Jenny files her nails.)

JENNY: And also, on top of all that? Her hand was damp.

(Imogene gives her the medicine.)

IMOGENE: You know Nurse Cathy's a virgin

DOVE: Nah

IMOGENE: It's true

DOVE: She's so old, though

MATHILDA: So?

IMOGENE: What?

MATHILDA: So what if she's a virgin?

IMOGENE: So there's nothing sadder than an adult virgin, obviously

MATHILDA: Oh.

(Maxx comes slamming in. She wears a knit cap that just screams teenage rebel, wears it with her uniform, she stomps onto the stage, turns a chair around and plops down, straddling it.
After a moment of people staring at her.)

MAXX: What?

JENNY: Nothing, you just seem so happy to be here.

(Maxx flips her off.)

DOVE: Didn't realize you were such a thespian, Maxx

MAXX: I'm not, I'm bi

IMOGENE: THESPIAN, stupid

MAXX: What's that

DOVE: Means you're into plays and shit

MAXX: Oh, yeah, no I'm not that either.
Sister Anne is making me do this bullshit.
To build my goddamn character or some stupid shit, fuck, I hate this goddamn fucking hellscape of a school!
(She looks at Mathilda who seems scandalized.)
WHAT?

MATHILDA: Nothing, nothing. I didn't say anything.

MAXX: Sister fucking Anne – she's such a cunt

MATHILDA: Oh.

(Maxx stares aggressively at Mathilda.)

MATHILDA: I don't know her, not really.
I mean, I only know her from the assembly.
And the morning announcements.
And she seems.
Okay!

MAXX: Whatever.

(Minnie enters.)

MINNIE: Sorry, I'm late, all! Was just printing out some – Where the fuck is everybody?

IMOGENE: We are the everybody.

MINNIE: No.

JENNY: Jesus, you don't have to sound so happy.

MINNIE: You all can't be it.

MAXX: We are

MINNIE: What, there's usually like twenty people who try out for drama!

DOVE: Yeah, when there's a normal play to try out for, when it's like *Peter Pan* or *The Sound of Music* or something people actually know about, nobody knows about your weird-ass shit.

MINNIE: Shut up, Dove

DOVE: I mean, shit, I'm only here 'cause mommy told me I had to be.

MINNIE: I'll tell her you said that, don't think I won't!

DOVE: It doesn't even have any singing in it, what kinda lame-ass play doesn't have singing in it??

MINNIE: Lots of plays don't have singing in them, Dove, you don't even know!

JENNY: Yeah, I mean, what is this even, you never really said...

MINNIE: I wrote a play! It's an adaptation of *Measure for Measure*.

JENNY: What's that?

MATHILDA: It's by William Shakespeare, one of his more controversial, problem plays

MINNIE: Yeah, it had problems all right, that's why I fixed them – it's for my senior thesis!

IMOGENE: Shit, you had to write a play and a paper?

MINNIE: No, just the play -

IMOGENE: Wait, what, you conned Sister Anne into letting you do a play instead of writing a paper for your senior thesis?!

JENNY: How'd you get away with that shit, I'll do it next year

IMOGENE: I would have done it this year, shit! Writing a play is like not hard

MINNIE: Yeah, okay.

IMOGENE: What, it's not! It's like one person talking then the next person talking and then another person talking and then a swordfight and then a chandelier falls and then people kiss and then it's over. I would have wrote a play if I knew it was an option!

MINNIE: Well, okay, sorry to burst your fucking bubble but ya didn't and also, by the way, it's not fucking easy, it's hard and it's stupid and I should have wrote a paper because there's not enough of you to even make the play work!

IMOGENE: What's it about?

MINNIE: I mean, it's mostly *Measure for Measure* but like. Set in hell.

I had to give it a religious bent for Sister Anne to give her stamp of approval and so I was like Well what if I like, set it in hell and we can see like how all the sinners are punished or whatever and she was like Sure and so it's basically like What happens after the original *Measure for Measure* ends and everyone's in hell getting tortured in different ways depending on what they did while they were alive, so it's that, and set in the future and in hell.

JENNY: How far in the future?

MINNIE: 2002.

DOVE: What future, that shit's now

MINNIE: I mean, it's set in the future now. It's Shakespeare-Future, but our now.

(They all let that sink in.)

IMOGENE: That's deep as fuck.

MINNIE: Yeah, I know!

DOVE: So wait, hold up, is it an adaptation or a sequel?

MINNIE: It's the same shit, Dove

DOVE: Uh, no, it's completely different, what are you telling me that like *Toy Story 2* is an adaptation of *Toy Story 1*?

MINNIE: Dove, I swear –

IMOGENE: Well, I think it sounds cool. And different. A whole play set in hell

MAXX: Don't that just make it set here.

MATHILDA: It's set in hell

MAXX: High school is hell. Earth is, too.

JENNY: For someone who doesn't like drama, you sure are dramatic

MAXX: Oh, I didn't realize that telling the truth was like a dramatic thing to do –

IMOGENE: You got the script, Minnie?

MINNIE: Yeah.

IMOGENE: Let's read it.

MINNIE: Yeah?

IMOGENE: Yeah, I mean, we're all here to do a play, right? So let's do it.

(A nice moment between the two of them.)

MATHILDA: Wait, aren't we going to audition? I've prepared several monologues –

IMOGENE: Yeah, we'll figure all that shit out, right, Minnie?

MINNIE: Yeah.
Yeah, exactly.
The play's the audition.
So like.
Let's go.

(She starts to hand out the scripts. While she does so, a chalkboard is rolled on and we enter into -)

SCENE II

(The words Sister Rose, World History 101 are written on it. Or maybe that's what SISTER ROSE *is writing as the chalkboard is rolled on.*
While this is happening, we still see the girls in the background on the stage, looking at their scripts and beginning to practice silently.
Sister Rose teaches history and she is very animated as she talks!)

SISTER ROSE: The year is 1524.
The place?
England.
The players – King Henry the VIII and Queen Anne Boleyan.
Now, who has heard of Queen Anne Boleyan, show of hands.
And what is she most known for?
What's that Nicole? Oh, I'm sorry, I thought you were talking to me, not Christina, my apologies, but Ladies, we are three days into the school year, if you can't even pretend to feign interest, then I dunno what to tell you!
Queen Anne is a remarkable figure! She is the reason for the destruction of the church in England! Yes, that's right, girls, one woman turned history on its head – which led her to losing hers!
(she laughs at her bad joke)
All right, enough funny business – it's 1524 and King Henry the VIII is unhappily married to his wife, Catharine but, as you all know, the Catholic Church does not recognize divorce – and what broke apart this union?
(she writes the word on the board:)
L-U-S-T.
(underlines it with a flourish.)
That's right, King Henry, rather than figuring out a way to make it work with Catherine, he creates his own church with his own rules so he can not only divorce his wife, but marry anew.
You see, ladies, lust makes us do crazy things. An entire system, destroyed in a moment all over a woman.
And speaking of women, for your first big project, I'm going to ask you to research into a famous woman and write all about her influences.
You're going to need access to the internet for this project.
Who doesn't have access to the internet?
All right, well, you're in luck! Because during the summer, I'm happy to share, the library has been freshly connected to the internet! So there will be no more excuses, everybody understand?
Good!
Now, turn to page twenty-seven in your textbooks and we'll really get going.

(The scene transforms to a library where we enter into -)

SCENE III

(Imogene and Minnie are in the library. Imogene is reading <u>Measure for Measure</u>. Minnie is writing her play.)

IMOGENE: Damn.

MINNIE: What.

IMOGENE: Nothing. I just. Can't believe Isabella wanted to be a nun that fucking bad.

MINNIE: Yeah, well –

IMOGENE: She was gonna fuck over her brother

MINNIE: Yeah, it's more complicated than that –

IMOGENE: Just to be a nun!
A fucking
NUN!
I mean, who wants to be a nun, even?!

MINNIE: I dunno, Imogene.
Probably just.
Every nun here?

IMOGENE: Oh yeah

MINNIE: Yeah.

IMOGENE: I dunno why.

MINNIE: Because it's a calling and shit

IMOGENE: I don't get it

MINNIE: Yeah that's because nobody's calling you.

(They go back to doing what they're doing.)

IMOGENE: Hey, why'd you choose this play?

MINNIE: You don't like it?

IMOGENE: No, I mean like - why not *Romeo and Juliet* or something we already did in class?

MINNIE: Oh. Because. I didn't want anything we had already done. I wanted to do something that nobody's ever done before so it could be me, all me. So I didn't even waste my time with the easy ones and I read all of them and Sister Ignatius was like Minnie, you're not gonna do *Titus Andronicus* so this one was the next best thing.

IMOGENE: Sister Ignatius is such a buzzkill.

MINNIE: She's not that bad.

IMOGENE: You kidding, she's always going around getting in everyone's business

MINNIE: Yeah well, she helped me out.
Last year.
When things got hard.
Because of my dad.
Not being there.

IMOGENE: Oh.

MINNIE: Yeah.

IMOGENE: I didn't know

MINNIE: Yeah because you weren't there, either.

IMOGENE: That's not fair

MINNIE: Yeah, right.

IMOGENE: You know why –

MINNIE: Not my fault I'm not gay –

IMOGENE: Yeah, I know!
I know and that's why.

I couldn't be around you.

MINNIE: Yeah, well, you missed out on a lot. So like.

(There's a moment of silence that passes between the two of them.)

MINNIE: She found me, once.
    In the cafeteria, last year after.
    Everything.
    I had gotten to school fine and was just sitting there and everyone was like…not seeing me? Like I was a ghost or something, like I was there but nobody could see me and the bell rang and everyone went to homeroom but me because I couldn't move, and I felt like I really was a ghost, maybe.
    Like, nothing felt real.
    And I was just.
    Sitting there.
    But Sister Ignatius, she saw me. She saw me and came over and she had chocolate milk.
    And some cookies.
    And she put them in front of me.
    And started talking to me like it was nothing.
    Like I wasn't supposed to be in homeroom.
    Like the day wasn't going on without me.
    She just started talking.
    And I slowly came back to life.

IMOGENE: Oh.

MINNIE: Yeah.

IMOGENE: I didn't know.

MINNIE: Obviously.

(Minnie goes back to writing. Imogene tries to say something but the words keep getting stuck to the roof of her mouth. She finally gets some of them out.)

IMOGENE: Hey. I'm glad we're friends again.

(Minnie looks at her. Nods her head a little.)

MINNIE: Yeah. I am, too.

(Music begins to play and we enter into –)

MOVEMENT II

(Minnie stands up and she starts to dance. Imogene and the world disappears as she dances and dances and –

she's getting really into it, dancing like nobody's watching. While she dances, she writes. We can't see what she's writing, but that's how she's writing, by dancing, her body are her words and the world is her page and she's filling it with her soul, she dance and dance until -)

SCENE IV

(Minnie is writing in her notebook on the stage, her music blasting so loud we can kinda hear it through her headphones. Dove enters the space, sees her across the room. She says her name over and over trying to get her attention until she's right up on her.)

DOVE: Minnie.
   Minnie.
   MINNIE!

(Dove nudges her sister with her foot and Minnie takes her headphones off.)

MINNIE: What!

DOVE: The fuck you mean What, I been waiting for you for a half hour!

MINNIE: I'm busy.

DOVE: It's time to go!

MINNIE: So go home, I'm in the zone.

DOVE: What zone are you in, please

MINNIE: You wouldn't get it

(She tries to put her headphones back on, but Dove interrupts.)

DOVE: I lost my metro card

MINNIE: That sounds like a You problem.

DOVE: Let me get yours

MINNIE: You don't have quarters?

DOVE: Used them all at lunch

MINNIE: Fine

(Gives her the card. Goes back to writing.)

DOVE: Have you ever dissected a frog?

MINNIE: Leave me alone

DOVE: It's important.

(beat)

MINNIE: Yeah.

DOVE: And?

MINNIE: And what, it was like cutting open a frog

DOVE: Ms. Diamantopoulos told us we're gonna do it in a couple of weeks.

MINNIE: So what's the problem?!

DOVE: I don't wanna do it

MINNIE: It's already dead when you get it

DOVE: But like…Ew.

MINNIE: I mean, it's just the insides, it's not like…like it doesn't bleed, you know? And you don't have to dissect it, who's your lab partner?

DOVE: Christina

MINNIE: Christina who

DOVE: Christina P

MINNIE: So just make her do it, you can just take the notes -

DOVE: What if she don't wanna??

MINNIE: I dunno what to tell you, Dove, you gotta grow up sometime.

(Dove lingers.)

DOVE: I memorized my lines.

MINNIE: For which scene

DOVE: For all of it

MINNIE: For real?

DOVE: Yeah.

MINNIE: Oh. Well, I'm changing most of it

DOVE: What?

MINNIE: Yeah, after the first rehearsal I was like Oh yeah this shit's bad so I'm changing it

DOVE: But I memorized all of it!

MINNIE: I dunno what you want me to tell you, Dove, I didn't tell you to memorize it and what am I supposed to do, just put up a shitty play, I don't think so. I mean, what do you think I'm doing now?

DOVE: You won't tell me.

MINNIE: I'm rewriting it.
And I was in the zone.
I dunno if I can get back there.

DOVE: Can't be too hard, if you were already there.

MINNIE: Yeah, I dunno.

(Another kind of beat shift.)

DOVE: Are you nervous?

MINNIE: We got 'til December to get it up, I'm sure it'll be fine –

DOVE: No, not about –

MINNIE: Then what -

DOVE: Tomorrow.

MINNIE: Oh. No.

DOVE: Yeah, me neither.

MINNIE: Nothing to be nervous about

DOVE: Right

MINNIE: We just gotta…Walk up to the stage when they say his name.

DOVE: Yeah.

MINNIE: That's all.

DOVE: And not cry, right?

MINNIE: You can cry.

DOVE: Oh yeah. But I won't.

MINNIE: Okay.

(She goes back to writing. But she doesn't put her headphones back on.)

DOVE: Christina says her dad thinks there's gonna be another attack.

MINNIE: I don't think so.

DOVE: Really?

MINNIE: Nah, makes no sense to do it again.
And we're safe out here.
So far out in Brooklyn?
Nothing's gonna get us out here.

DOVE: Promise?

MINNIE: Sure.

(There's a nice moment between the two of them.)

DOVE: Daddy's probably in hell, right?

(That changes the mood. Minnie turns into a storm cloud.)

MINNIE: Go away, Dove.

DOVE: No, I just mean - because he was gonna leave mommy and I thought – that maybe that's why you're writing the play, because of that and the last time -

MINNIE: Well, I'm not, Dove, I'm writing the play because I didn't wanna write a paper and I just thought it would be a cool thing to do and I'm not writing it because of Daddy and I don't care where Daddy is right now 'cause he isn't here, so just shut up about it and leave me alone.

*(Minnie leaves. Dove is alone. As the scene begins to change around her.
Sister Ignatius appears, standing at a podium. We hear her say the ceremony and just watch Dove react on the stage, though it's not in real time.)*

SISTER IGNATIUS: …Michael Jones, remembered by his cousin, Nicole Andrews.
Stephanie Rogers, remembered by her niece, Vanessa Rivera.
And Robin Greene, remembered by his daughters, Minerva and Dove Greene.
We remember those who were taken, one year ago today, and pray that the Lord is cradling them in His arms.
And so we sing.

(She begins to lead everyone in a song like "On Eagle's Wings." Dove stays on the stage, maybe she mouths along with the words, as the scene shifts to after school the same day in -)

SCENE V

(The auditorium again, after school. Dove and Mathilda are rehearsing by themselves.
Well, they should be – Dove is reading through her lines and Mathilda is staring out the window.
We can't see them, but there's a gaggle of guys from St. Timothy's all standing outside, kinda staring at the school.
It's a daily occurrence when school is in session but this is the first Mathilda is seeing of it.)

DOVE: I'll be ready in a second

MATHILDA: Oh, sure.
　(beat)
　Do they always just.
　Stand there?

DOVE: What?
　Oh, yeah.
　You'll get used to it.

MATHILDA: Oh.

DOVE: Seriously, don't let them bother you, most of them have got girlfriends they're waiting for. The rest are just thirsty.

MATHILDA: Where do they. Come from?

DOVE: Oh, St. Timothy's, it's like four or five blocks away or something?

MATHILDA: Ah.

DOVE: But it doesn't matter, seriously.
Besides, we've gotta practice.
They'll definitely be gone by the time we're done.
You don't have to be so nervous

MATHILDA: I'm not nervous.
It's just.
Creepy.
Don't you think it's creepy?

DOVE: I dunno, it's just kinda….Normal.

MATHILDA: Okay.

(Dove decides to try to make small talk.)

DOVE: So. How're you finding shit otherwise?

MATHILDA: It's all. Fine. I guess.

DOVE: Yeah, it's a lot to get used to, but don't worry, you'll get used to it. Then you can act like you're the queen of shit just like Imogene and my sister, Seniors are the fucking worst.

MATHILDA: Yeah, they really are.

DOVE: I can't wait to be a senior.

MATHILDA: I can't wait to.
Not be a Freshman.

DOVE: Yeah.
That shit was rough.
Sophomore year is better, swear.

MATHILDA: Okay.

(beat)

MATHILDA: Hey, uh, so I didn't know your dad died in nine-eleven.

DOVE: Yeah.

MATHILDA: I'm sorry.

DOVE: You didn't do it.

MATHILDA: I know.
 Just...it must be hard.

DOVE: It sucks, yeah.
 It was my first day of high school.
 Last year.

MATHILDA: Oh.
 That seems like.
 It would've been rough.

DOVE: Yeah.

MATHILDA: My first day was.
 Not great!
 But.
 It wasn't like that.

DOVE: Yeah, I bet it wasn't.

MATHILDA: I wasn't even here yet, when it happened?
 I was still in Michigan

DOVE: Michigan

MATHILDA: Yeah, that's where I'm from, really? But my mom got transferred and we were all set to move here but then it happened and they were like Oh should we still move and then we did. And now I'm here.

DOVE: Yeah that's like.
Super brave of you and your entire family.

MATHILDA: Oh, it's not that – *(she realizes that she was making fun of her. Kinda shuts up for a second.)* The ceremony was nice today.

DOVE: I guess.

MATHILDA: You got a rose.

DOVE: Yeah, so what, I already threw it out.
Smashed up the petals and threw them in the trash.

MATHILDA: Oh.

DOVE: Fuck roses, they just die.
Stupid to have a remembrance or whatever if it's just gonna die.
They're big on roses here.

MATHILDA: Probably because of Mary.

DOVE: What about Mary?

MATHILDA: It's like…how she's represented.
A bunch of the saints – the female saints – St. Rose.
Obviously.
And St. Therese, too.

DOVE: Oh. I didn't know that.

MATHILDA: Yeah.
My mom, actually,
she does these things called Novenas?
It's a buncha specific kinda prayers that you do over the course of nine days –
it's really important for it to be nine days for some reason -
and you can pray them to a buncha different saints but she likes to do them to St. Therese because at the end of the cycle, you'll know if your prayer comes true because on the tenth day somehow, during your day, when you least expect it, there'll be roses.
Somewhere.
I like it because it feels like magic.
I mean, I know we're not supposed to believe in magic but.

Sometimes I dunno what the difference is between what Jesus did and magic.
I kinda think sometimes that maybe.
Maybe they're the same thing.
Just different words for the same thing.

DOVE: That's actually.
Cool.

MATHILDA: Yeah?!

DOVE: Yeah.
Some sorta magic.
Cool.

MATHILDA: Cool!
Are you ready to rehearse?

DOVE: Yeah, I guess.
Might as well get it over with.

MATHILDA: I actually really like it!
Your sister did a good job.

DOVE: It's okay, I guess.

MATHILDA: It's interesting.
I'm really bummed that Isabella's not in it, though, but I get it, she wouldn't be in hell, you know?

DOVE: Uh, not really, since I don't really know the play?

MATHILDA: Oh, yeah, she is tasked with the greatest moral decision of the play, Angelo, this corrupt guy, he puts these really strict rules in place about [*whisper/mutters*] sex [*regular voice*] and stuff, and Isabella's brother Claudio is sentenced to death for impregnating his fiancée and Angelo tells her she can save him if they just have sex and she refuses because her faith and morals are so important to her, she's unwavering.
So that's why she's not in hell.
Because she did the right thing.

DOVE: Uh huh.

MATHILDA: If we were doing the real play, I would've wanted to be Isabella.
I can relate to her.
Not that they would've given that role to a Freshman but.
Still.

DOVE: Well.
It's good to have goals, right?
Come on.
Let's practice.

(They stand in front of one another each do a little actor Getting into the zone! thing before they begin.)

DOVE: *(in character)* Hey, Mariana!
It's me, Juliet!
Doth your eyes recognize me?

MATHILDA: *(in character)* Juliet, I remember a Juliet.
You are like a beacon of light,
Cutting the darkness in half!
How lovely it is to see you here.

(As they continue to practice, another chalkboard is rolled on and we are in -)

SCENE VI

(The chalkboard says SISTER LUCY – ADV. CHEM. *and contains some complex looking chemistry equations on it. Sister Lucy is less theatrical than Sister Rose in her lessons, but she is pretty brilliant and smart.)*

SISTER LUCY: All right, Class, it sounds like we can all stand to have a refresher –
Now, there are three physical states of Matter –
Solids.
Liquids.
And Gases.
Anything in this world that occupies any kind of space is composed of Matter and -

Yes, Kimberlee? Uh huh. Uh huh.
Well, sure, you can't always see Gas but matter in a gaseous state is still taking up space. Yes, it still is, even if it's not something you can see with the human eye.
Everything, from the mountains to a breadcrumb, as long as it takes up space, it is composed of Matter and so, it matters.
All of you, girls, you are composed of Matter.
But you don't just fill space with your bodies, you also contain your souls. And just because you can't see your souls, that doesn't mean they're not there, right?
Maybe they're not officially a type of matter because we don't know what form they exist in, but as long as they're attached to your body, you enter into space with them and – I think that matters.
Because you matter.
You take up space.
And you should.
You all should take up as much space as you can. With your voices, heart, brains, selves.
I think all of that might be matter, too.
Now, please turn to chapter 5 in your textbooks – and Yes, this all will be on the test so pay attention, please.

(We transition to -)

SCENE VII

(Imogene is standing on the stage. She's practicing as well as she can without a scene partner.)

IMOGENE: *(as Claudio in hell)* Tell me, Devil, [*as herself*]
No....
(back in character)
Devil have you...*(can't remember the words.)*
(tries again)
Devil! Have you...seen....
(she's like Fuck it and takes out her script, jogs her memory-mind.)
Okay
(back in character)
Tell me, Devil,
have you seen my sister?
I'm newly tortured here.

Her name is Isabella.
Has her body been made food for worms?
Does she have a bunk down here in this wasteland of tortured souls
or is she still living on Earth?
Or will her soul soar up to Heaven?
(as herself)
This is so stupid.
Nobody talks like this!
God.
(as the Devil)
Uh, blahblahblah, I dunno,
Something like what makes you think I'm gonna tell you,
I'm literally the Devil.
(as Claudio)
Surely there's a way to know!

(Jenny enters.)

JENNY: Sorry -

IMOGENE: Yo, what the fuck

JENNY: Sorry, sorry -

IMOGENE: I've been waiting –

JENNY: I know, I'm sure –

IMOGENE: everyone else's been working on their scenes and I'm over here talking to myself like I know what I'm doing, I dunno what I'm doing -

JENNY: I know, Jesus, Imogene!
I already said sorry, what else do you want from me, blood?

IMOGENE: That's okay.

JENNY: Good.

(beat)

IMOGENE: You ready to rehearse or what?

JENNY: Yeah, no, sorry, I was just.
　I had a kinda.
　Long day.

IMOGENE: Use it in the scene

JENNY: It's so stupid

IMOGENE: Tell me, I like stupid

JENNY: I was.
　With Nurse Cathy

IMOGENE: More cramps?

JENNY: No I –
　I kinda threw up

IMOGENE: What, ew, are you okay?!

JENNY: Yeah it was
　So dumb!
　And like, gross, it smelled and it was orange and you could still kinda see chunks of fritos

IMOGENE: Oh my god, don't describe it!

JENNY: in fucking biology I had to cut up an earthworm.

IMOGENE: Oh yeah, I remember earthworm day!
　That shit was nasty.

JENNY: Yeah.

IMOGENE: Yeah, it had to do a lot with its anus or some shit

JENNY: Uh huh

IMOGENE: Yeah, I was like Okay, yeah, I appreciate doing this but I'm definitely gonna go out of my way to do a job where I'll literally never have to do this again. It was pretty gross.

JENNY: Sure, but, okay,
    I wasn't grossed out, though,
    seriously, it was that.
    I just.
    I didn't know that they were so.
    Full.

IMOGENE: What do you mean?

JENNY: I dunno, they're just bugs, you know?
    But they have this whole.
    Ecosystem of life inside them.
    Keeping them alive.
    I just never really.
    Thought about it before.
    Like, it had a digestive system.
    And a blood vessel.
    And a whole system of nerves just woven through them

IMOGENE: Jenny.
    It's not that serious.
    It's not like they can think or anything –

JENNY: But they can feel, pain and -

IMOGENE: But they don't really have lives, you know?
    Their lives are just being worms,
    eating dirt and shitting it back out,
    that's not really much of a life-life, you know?

JENNY: They have hearts. Like, more than one heart.

IMOGENE: Yeah, and?

JENNY: That means they can love.
    I mean, they have more than one heart, beating inside them, it
    probably means they can double love and love so deep and -

IMOGENE: All right, listen, no.
    I never heard any scientific evidence that love is stored in our
    heart.
    That's just some Hallmark Corporation made up bullshit,
    for all we know, we keep our love stored in our tits.
    Or our noses.

Or eyes.
Or maybe we keep it stored in our entire bodies,
and our love runs through us and just knows no end.

(There's a quiet, tender, intimate moment that passes between the two of them.)

IMOGENE: Anyway.
I dunno what I'm talking about –

JENNY: We keep our love in our hands.

IMOGENE: See?
Earthworms don't have hands

JENNY: That's right, they don't.

IMOGENE: I think it's sweet.
That you care about earthworms.

(They get closer and closer.)

JENNY: Nah.
I'm just being stupid.

IMOGENE: I don't think you are.
I actually.
I think you're one of the sweetest people I know.

(They're still looking at one another as their hands slowly start to dance towards one another.)

JENNY: I dunno.

*(Slowly, very slowly, they hold hands.
A moment goes by.
They hold hands tighter.
Minnie comes in.
They shoot apart but she saw them.)*

MINNIE: Hey, uh.
How's that scene coming?

JENNY & IMOGENE: Good, good, it's great

MINNIE: Okay, can I see?

JENNY: No, uh, I actually – I think I've gotta, I gotta go…

MINNIE: Rehearsal's not done –

JENNY: Yeah, no, I'm just – I don't think I'm feeling a hundred percent, my stomach – I gotta...

(she leaves. Imogene looks after her.)

IMOGENE: *(an explanation)* She threw up earlier so.

MINNIE: Hey.
Uh.
You…okay?

IMOGENE: Yeah, of course.

MINNIE: Lost your scene partner –

IMOGENE: Yeah, I'm used to it.

(She starts to gather her stuff. Minnie comes over to her.)

MINNIE: I'll do the scene with you.

IMOGENE: You don't hafta.

MINNIE: Nah, come on.
Let's do it.

(Imogene looks at Minnie.)
IMOGENE: Tell me Devil.
I'm newly tortured here.

(End scene.)

SCENE VIII

(During that same rehearsal, but in a different area, a classroom that the three have taken over for rehearsal, Mathilda, Maxx and Dove rehearse.)

MATHILDA: ...and so your character's probably in hell because even though he technically didn't do anything wrong in *Measure for Measure*, because he didn't actually go through with having sex with Isabella which woulda been really bad, he just had sex with Mariana *(gestures to herself because she's playing Mariana)* and Mariana was technically, they were supposed to be married so even though they...you knowhadsexorwhatever, it wasn't as big enough deal to be put to death because of the Duke, BUT he was kind of morally in the wrong, you know?

(They both kinda stare at her.)

MAXX: You know a lot about this lameass play.

MATHILDA: My father's actually, he's a Shakespeare scholar? So he's been helping me in his spare time -

DOVE: Wait, so why's my character in hell, then?

MATHILDA: I uh, I'm actually not sure – I mean, Juliet was impregnated by Claudio but they get married and it's fine in the end and I think your sister just like...wanted to make it work so she stuck everyone in hell

DOVE: Yeah, that makes sense.

MAXX: This shit's so absurd.
Like, this whole concept is whack.
There's no such thing as hell.

DOVE: You don't think so?

MATHILDA: I mean. It is in the bible.

MAXX: So what?
Lots of shit's in the bible.
Doesn't make it true.
Like, by their own rules, all the nuns at this spot?
Would be going to hell if they played that close to the rules.

MATHILDA: No

DOVE: Oh shit, you're right

MAXX: I know!

MATHILDA: Why?!

DOVE: Because!
This whole place used to be a place of sin!
It was a brothel.

MATHILDA: No.

MAXX: Deadass.

DOVE: Yeah. I mean, it didn't start off like that, it was this rich guy's wife's spot but then she died and his mistress moved in and she was a savvy businesswoman so she was like Hun, you know this big ol' house, just sitting here, gathering dust? And he was like yeah and she was like Wattaya say we fill it? And he said As long's you give me a cut, sure, and so that's what she did and it was a bustling brothel for years til they were going bankrupt and then the sisters came in and bought it from them and then boom.
Catholic school.

MATHILDA: They left that part off the tour.

DOVE: Yeah, they like to pretend it didn't happen but it did so we all always find out and pass it down.

MATHILDA: It could just be a story.

MAXX: Yeah but it's not.
Sometimes, late at night, you can still hear the sounds of men cumming echoing off the lockers that line these lonely halls.
(She makes some orgasm sounds.)

DOVE: *(Also makes some orgasm sounds.)*

(Mathilda laughs politely.)

DOVE: And in religion we're doing morality and Sister Ignatius SAID that like if you get donations that you know have been gotten by "evils means" then it's IMMORAL to accept them!

And the point of things being moral or IMMORAL is for God to decide whether or not you're going to Heaven or Hell. Right?

MATHILDA: I mean, it's more complicated than that -

MAXX: Hell is just all stories to scare people into not dying. And to be nice while we're alive.

MATHILDA: I'm not.
I don't think that's true

MAXX: Sure, it might not be true.
And it might be true.
We don't know.
That's the point, we don't know.
We don't know if it all stops or starts or doesn't or does, we don't know. But sometimes living on earth can be hell. Sometimes living on earth can feel like a never ending hellscape and sometimes that really sucks and sometimes I wonder if death is hell or if it's just nothing, if it's just that everything stops and.
Then, I dunno.
It's weird being alive.

MATHILDA: That's a weird thing to say

MAXX: No, but really, it is, weird being alive. None of us asked to be alive, you know? We were all just given life and put on this fucking little ball of blue and it's full of all these people who all want to take us and put us into boxes and.
I dunno.
That kinda sucks, doesn't it?
That none of us asked for this but they all get these ideas about how to be right
and how to be wrong.
Sometimes I wonder.
No.
Sometimes I think.
That maybe if there weren't all these people trying to tell us about all the wrong,
that maybe then, it might be easier to wanna be alive.

MATHILDA: I dunno, I think being alive is pretty great.

MAXX: You would.
   You follow the rules.
   You fit into the rulebook.
   You can walk around freely, knowing that as long as you keep on following those rules, you belong.
   I don't belong.
   And I never will.

MATHILDA: Well, I dunno.
   Maybe you just need to.
   Pray.

(The two of them look at her in disbelief and then they start to laugh.)

MAXX: Oh yeah, all the prayers, they sure did fix everything, don't they?

DOVE: Yeah, I dunno why I didn't think've that.

MAXX: Was I ever that young as a Freshman?

DOVE: I don't think I was ever that young when I was young, shit.

MATHILDA: No but.
   Doesn't it bring you comfort?
   To talk to God?
   He's always listening –

MAXX: Nah.
   That shit don't bring me comfort.
   Actually, nothing does.

(She packs her shit and leaves.
Dove leaves, too.
Mathilda stands there.
Church music begins to play and we enter into -)

SCENE IX

(In the lunchroom.
Maxx is sitting by herself, reading something like the Complete Works of Fredrich Nietzsche.
Imogene is sitting across the cafeteria also eating by herself but looking up for someone.
Jenny walks by, holding a tray.
Imogene waves to her but Jenny pretends not to see her – not in a bitchy way but in a way that she's still confused about what happened between the two of them so truly acting like she doesn't see her.
She sees Maxx and slides into the seat.
Imogene is dejected but stays at her table.)

JENNY: Oh hey!

MAXX: ...what?

JENNY: Nothing, hi!

MAXX: I'm reading.

JENNY: I didn't realize we had lunch together.

MAXX: Yeah, because you're usually with Imogene in your own little world together –

JENNY: I wouldn't say –
I think we're in the same world, honestly –

MAXX: Sure.

(A moment of silence goes by.)

JENNY: What did you bring for lunch?

MAXX: We don't have to talk.

JENNY: Okay.
Your book looks intense.

(Maxx gives up.)

MAXX: Something on your mind?

JENNY: No.

MAXX: Right.

JENNY: No.
It's just that.
Something kinda.
Happened.
The other day.

MAXX: Okay.

JENNY: And I like.
I dunno
Just.
Can I ask you something?

MAXX: Jesus Christ, just do it

JENNY: How did you know you liked.
Both guys and girls.

MAXX: Because.
I like both guys and girls.

JENNY: Okay, never mind.

MAXX: No, I mean.
I dunno, how do you describe something you just know is true?

JENNY: But.
How do you *know*?

MAXX: There's no answers for shit like this.
It just is what it is.
Do you like Imogene or not?

JENNY: She's my best friend.

MAXX: Yeah, and?

JENNY: I mean.
I kinda do.

MAXX: Okay then!

JENNY: But I've only liked boys before –

MAXX: God, who cares!
I don't gotta educate you on this shit.
Leave me alone.

JENNY: Damn, Maxx, why do you always have to be so angry?
The world's not always out to get you, shit.

MAXX: Would you even be talking to me if we weren't doing the school play together?
Or would I just be the same Loser as I was last year?

JENNY: I literally never called you a loser –

MAXX: "Literally" you did, and it's still up in the bathroom so don't go acting like you're the queen of shit now, I can see directly through your bullshit and I don't need you to feel like you gotta be my friend and I definitely don't need to bond with you over any shit but ESPECIALLY not over the fact you don't know whether or not you got a crush on your best friend. I'm out.

(She leaves.
Jenny looks across the cafeteria.
Imogene looks back.
Jenny gets up, begins to walk towards her but
then she decides to leave.)

SCENE X

(The scene transforms to the auditorium but during the day –
There's a special presentation with an outside person! There's a PowerPoint set up that says Your Body and You! MRS. O'DONELL stands in front of it, beaming at the girls, she's more of a salesperson than a caring body positive person.)

MRS. O'DONELL: Hello, Our Lady of Sorrows! Thank you so much for having me today, my   name is Mrs. O'Donell and I'm here today to talk with you about something I think we can all relate to –
Menstruation!
(She clicks a clicker and the slide changes to say Menstruation!)
Now, who here started getting their period when they were fourteen, show of hands?
Okay, and thirteen?
Twelve? *(She raises her hand)*
Eleven?
(She clicks a clicker and the slide changes to show a chart with different ages to show how many people on average get periods and when.)
Did you know there is no Right age to get your period? Girls have gotten periods as young as nine and as old as sixteen! It's true! Your body is its own clock, internally clicking and only your body knows when to set that alarm off and start the flow and when to turn it off.
We know so much more about the female body in 2002 than we ever have before!
And yet we don't know everything.
And I'm sure there's some things that are even a mystery to all of you.
Now.
Who can tell me how many holes we have in our bodies?
(She listens.)
Uh huh, uh huh, I'm hearing a lot of twos out there and some threes.
Well, the correct answer is –
(She changes a slide to show a diagram of a body with a reproductive system which shows three holes – urethra, anus and vagina.)
Three!
There's, of course, the anus, and we all know what that's for, but what a lot of young women don't realize is that the hole you urinate from is actually different from the hole you menstruate from – it's actually quite common to think that –
(She stops because she sees something.)
All right, it looks like we've got a fainter, it's all right girls, everyone, give her some air!

(we transition into -)

SCENE XI

(After school, at play rehearsal. The girls are gathering. Minnie is trying to get things in order.)

MINNIE: No, Jenny.

JENNY: Yo, just hear me out!

MINNIE: I'm not putting a randomass dance number in it just because you wanna dance!

JENNY: But why not though!

MINNIE: Because they're all in hell!
Everyone's in hell!
This is a play that takes place in literally HELL,
why're they gonna be doing a dance in HELL, Jenny?!
That shit makes no sense.

JENNY: Yo, use your imagination

MINNIE: What do you think I'm doing?! This whole THING is my imagination!

JENNY: Your imagination doesn't contain music?

MINNIE: No.

JENNY: Pretty lame imagination then.

DOVE: Minnie, I got a question –

MINNIE: Go ask the Encyclopedia

DOVE: It's about the play

MINNIE: Fine, what.

(They huddle together while Jenny goes and pouts to Imogene. Imogene nudges Jenny.)

IMOGENE: Hey.

JENNY: (*Looks at her like what.*)

IMOGENE: I think you should dance.

JENNY: Yeah, okay.

IMOGENE: Seriously.

JENNY: Whatever.

IMOGENE: Yo.
Are we cool?
I miss you.

DOVE: You can't just CUT my CHARACTER

MINNIE: You'll still be IN the play -

DOVE: But I was Juliet!

MINNIE: Yeah and I realized that it didn't make sense to have her be in HELL, she didn't do anything wrong so.

DOVE: God!

MINNIE: Don't worry, you'll still have lines or whatever, you can be the lead hell ensemble member – and you can do props -

DOVE: Whatever, it doesn't matter, shit.

(*She sits down, looking at her new script and pouting.*)

MINNIE: All right, we really gotta get started –
Anybody know where Mathilda's at?

MAXX: Probably still with Nurse Cathy

JENNY: What happened, she ok?

MAXX: I dunno, she kinda wiped out during assembly today

MINNIE: What assembly?

DOVE: You wouldn't know about it, it was just for the Freshmen and Sophomores

IMOGENE: Oh, with the Tampon Lady

JENNY: I remember that shit

MINNIE: They still let the tampon lady in here?

MAXX: Uh yeah

JENNY: Yooo, tampons can literally kill you

MAXX: They can NOT

JENNY: Yes, they can! It happened to this girl that my cousin's sister went to school with!

IMOGENE: You're lying

DOVE: Nah, it's true, I read a thing about it in YM

MAXX: Yeah, well, I don't read YM

JENNY: Yeah, okay, then why'd they write about it if it's not true then

MAXX: I dunno, I don't work for YM!

JENNY: You can die from tampons, it's a real thing, it's a truth, Sister Lucy told me

DOVE: Sister LUCY told you

JENNY: Yeah, I mean she gets a period, too, right?!

MAXX: Sister Lucy probably thinks that using a tampon means she gonna lose her virginity

JENNY: Wait, but.
Isn't that true?

MINNIE: You can't break your hymen from a TAMPON

JENNY: I mean, technically –

IMOGENE: Breaking your hymen isn't the only way you can lose your virginity –

JENNY & DOVE & MINNIE: What?

MAXX: All right, okay, if tampons can murder you then why am I not dead right now? I've got one in CURRENTLY. And I'm ALIVE.

DOVE: Okay, ew

MAXX: What?

DOVE: We don't need to know that much of your business right now!

MAXX: God, whatever!
Anyway, the Tampon Lady was up there, giving her presentation about vaginas and shit and Mathilda just fainted in front of the whole school

MINNIE: Whoa

DOVE: I mean, it was pretty warm in there, I was getting warm, too -

MAXX: She's such a baby, like such an innocent baby that she can't even take the fact that she gets a period, like, how sad is that?

IMOGENE: Yeah, that's crazy

MAXX: I mean, she was trying to leave all stealthy like, right? But she had to make it through a row of people, she was sitting dead center, and she like wound up wiping OUT, like she tripped over people's legs and slid into the side and the floor was slippery so it was just like watching a rag doll bang into the wall, it was wild, it was totally wild.

(Mathilda has entered and overhears all this.
People are laughing.
It hurts her.)

MINNIE: Oh shit, Mathilda

MATHILDA: Hi

MINNIE: You good?

MATHILDA: No.
   No, actually.
   I'm not good at all.
   I'd better.
   I'm just gonna go.
   I'm gonna go.

MINNIE: Mathilda, wait –

(She leaves.)

MINNIE: Did you really have to do that?

MAXX: What?
   Not my fault my shit's too real for her virgin ears!
   Damn.

MINNIE: It's not that big a deal

MAXX: You were laughing, too!

IMOGENE: I'm sure she'll come back.
   Like, tomorrow or whatever.
   She loves this stupi-she loves this play.

MINNIE: Shit, I guess.
   Dove.
   You're the understudy now.
   All right, everyone, let's.
   Let's get to work.

(They get into position, begin rehearsing silently, while the next scene sets up.)

SCENE XII.

(Sister Ignatius' office. She sits at her desk, grading papers. She takes a break. Rubs her temple. She picks up her pen again. Stops. Picks up her cross. Holds it a moment, looking at it. Closes her eyes and prays. Imogene knocks and startles her.)

IMOGENE: Hey Sister Ignatius, you wanted to see me?

SISTER IGNATIUS: Oh yes, yes -

IMOGENE: Sorry, were you sleeping?
 I can come back if now's not a good -

SISTER IGNATIUS: I was praying - Come, have a seat.

(Imogene sits.)

IMOGENE: I'm sorry, am I in trouble, or…?

SISTER IGNATIUS: No, no, not at all.
 Just thought it might be nice if we had a little.
 Check in.
 I do this with all the seniors – making sure you're on track for wrapping up your year.

IMOGENE: Oh, well, yeah, cool.
 Well yeah, I think everything's going according to plan – been doing college applications, play rehearsal –

SISTER IGNATIUS: Yes, how is the play going?

IMOGENE: Oh, it's good.
 It's great, actually.
 Minnie's a really good writer.

SISTER IGNATIUS: Wonderful, wonderful.
 And your classes?

IMOGENE: First quarter grades are mostly A's and B's.
 Applying to honors programs at a bunch of CUNY schools like Brooklyn College and Hunter and stuff so I can like,

live at home, maybe work on the side or whatever. I really like history so was kinda thinking of majoring in that.
Be nice to stay close to home.
Be near friends.

SISTER IGNATIUS: Like Jenny.

IMOGENE: Sure.
Like Jenny.
And Minnie.
And whoever.

SISTER IGNATIUS: Well, I'm glad to hear that your senior year is progressing smoothly. Though I have noticed that you've stopped participating in mass.

IMOGENE: Yeah.

SISTER IGNATIUS: And confession, too

IMOGENE: I've got nothing to confess.
So.
I stopped going.
That's all.

SISTER IGNATIUS: Are you a perfect human, Imogene?

IMOGENE: Well, yeah.

SISTER IGNATIUS: You're perfect

IMOGENE: No I'm not perfect but
I am a perfect human.
Because to be a human means to be flawed.
And I'm flawed as fu-heck.
I'm full of flaws.
Therefore, I am being as human as we come.
And even more therefore.
I am perfectly human.
A perfect human.

(A beat. Sister Ignatius smiles.)

SISTER IGNATIUS: That's clever.

IMOGENE: It's true

SISTER IGNATIUS: Imogene, do you know what confession is?

IMOGENE: Yeah, asking for forgiveness.

SISTER IGNATIUS: Do you know what a sin is?

IMOGENE: Yeah, of course –

SISTER IGNATIUS: Every time you break the divine law, another sin sits on top of your soul like dirt, gathering like dust bunnies under a bed, but confession, a simple act of confessing your sins and asking for forgiveness, it washes them all away, washes your soul clean until it's sparkling again. If a soul remains filthy with sin, it begins to rot. And I don't want that to happen to you.

IMOGENE: What do you mean -

SISTER IGNATIUS: Imogene.
I'm not like the other Sisters.
I know.
It's not a choice.
Who you are.

IMOGENE: Really?

SISTER IGNATIUS: Yes.
Of course, I know.
But.
It is a choice what you do.

IMOGENE: I don't.
What do you –

SISTER IGNATIUS: There are two mourning doves that have made a home inside my air conditioner.

IMOGENE: Okay.

SISTER IGNATIUS: They usually breed in spring, but
   sometimes they wait until the fall, even
   as the fall begins to turn to winter.
   They've been nice to come home to.
   I've been watching them, the two of them, the pair of them,
   tend to their nest.
   Have seen their little eggs.
   Together they brought life into this world.
   They couldn't have done that if they were both female
   mourning doves.
   Do you understand what I'm saying?
   I understand that it might be who you are but
   you understand that it's not part of our nature, don't you?
   We look to nature to understand our nature.
   That's where we find what's natural.
   Who you are is not the sin.
   But what you do, that is the sin.

IMOGENE: But who I am –
   It's who I am and -

SISTER IGNATIUS: Just look to the animals.
   That's where we understand what is right.
   And what is wrong.
   And think about going to confession.
   All right?

(Imogene slowly nods her head because she doesn't know what else to do.)

SISTER IGNATIUS: Good. You may leave now.

(But Imogene- doesn't leave – the world moves around her instead.
She stands frozen in place while the world moves around her, there should be elements of slow-mo as the world moves around her, and faster pace, something to make it clear that she feels like the world is moving and moving and moving until she bursts into the chapel/auditorium and starts her speech.)

IMOGENE: Dear Lord God in Heaven.
   What the actual
   Fuck?

I know you just saw that shit go down with Sister Ignatius and I.
I.
Fuck.
FUCK.
She just.
And I.
And I didn't say anything.
I just let her say.
All that and.
I shoulda said something,
I shoulda said like FUCK YOU!
Or just That's not true or.
Something.
"Look to nature to understand our nature" when she's out there saying she KNOWS that I'm like this and –
"Look to our nature to understand our nature" what fucking nature is that.
I thought we was supposed to be like...more than the animals.
God, I just thought you made it so we'd more than the animals.
Not better than the animals but like More.
So doesn't that mean we get to be more?
More complicated, more More, just like.
More.
But if she's calling me in, telling me that it's not like... right to be me, doesn't that mean she's calling me a sin?
That I'm a sin?
I'm a...sin.

(Jenny comes in and watches as Imogene continues to talk to God.)

IMOGENE: Love is like. A really fucking huge, complicated thing and I'm pretty sure animals don't love one another. They don't go around, asking one another out on dates – they don't even ask for permission to fuck, they just fuck one another because they have something inside of them that's saying Survive, Survive, don't go extinct, do whatever you gotta do to survive.
 – and I'm supposed to want to be that?
I'm supposed to want to emulate the animals when I'm a

human?
With a multi-faceted soul and like so many complexities, I'm not even aware of all of them and they just want to survive but we.
Humans, we.
We get to Live.
We get to Be.
You made us to be more than the animals, God.
And I'm over here, falling in love with people who aren't gonna love me back and losing my best friends in the process and.
Am I a sin, God?

(Jenny approaches Imogene.
She holds her hand.
Imogene is startled.
Sees her.
Holds her hand back.
Jenny slowly kisses Imogene.
They kiss quickly but
then they hug.

As they continue to hug, Minnie appears in another section of the stage.)

MINNIE: You wanted to see me, Sister?

(The lights go down and we

End Act I)

ACT II

SCENE I

(The auditorium, after school. They're only a couple of weeks away from the big play and they are all FEELING! THE! PRESSURE!)

JENNY: *(as the Devil)* But Mariana, you dared tarnish your virtue by sleeping with Angelo and henceforth you…You… Line.

DOVE: It's not….You're not even close to the line, you're in a different scene

JENNY: SERIOUSLY?!

DOVE: Yeah, you're really bad at this.

JENNY: Shit, I know! It's hard to memorize shit when there's no singing. Fuck.

MATHILDA: I think you're doing a great job, Jenny

JENNY: I'm dragging us all down but okay

IMOGENE: Fuck, who's read The Crucible?

JENNY: I've literally never even heard of it

IMOGENE: Sister Benedict assigned it and it's like – Nobody speaks real English in it, it's whack, I don't understand a word they say. *(To Mathilda)* Hey – who do you have for Lit?

MATHILDA: Oh, uh, Sister Agnes

JENNY: Oh, you're lucky

IMOGENE: She's easy

MATHILDA: Yeah?

JENNY: Yeah, her quizzes are dumb, she likes to spell shit out with her multiple-choice answers

DOVE: Wait, are you serious?

JENNY: Yeah, what, you never noticed?

DOVE: No!

IMOGENE: Why do you think she gives 5 choices for each, it's so she's got another vowel to play with

DOVE: You gotta be kidding

IMOGENE: Nah, deadass!

DOVE: Fuck English, I hate books. Math's where it's at.

JENNY: *(To Mathilda)* What book're you on?

MATHILDA: Oh, uh, Catcher and the Rye

MAXX: I fucking love that book.
Holden Caulfield is so real.

JENNY: Yeah, I liked that one!

DOVE: We're reading The Scarlet Letter

JENNY: Oh shit, with Sister Theresa?

DOVE: Yeah

IMOGENE: She still teaching that shit?!
She HATES Hester

(The girls all burst into laughter.)

JENNY: Oh my god, I know, right? She like really hates her, she likes, brings it up in casual conversation how much she hates Heater, I dunno why she teaches it

MAXX: I think she likes being angry, or like, getting to put her anger all on one person, right –

IMOGENE: *(as Sister Theresa)* She is a SINNER, GIRLS. She is a SINNER and her soul will rot with all the fire of that the eternal damnation of hell can muster and don't think it won't happen to you if you decide to go down that path! *(as herself)* Like that bitch is a real human person, please, she is a made-up book character! Like, chill!

(All the girls keep laughing.)

JENNY: Hey, you ever notice that like, most've the books we're reading are like men being heroic and shit but the one that's about the woman is like.
Not.
That?

(A pause, the laughter dies. As it does, Minnie enters. She stands and watches the girls for a moment.)

JENNY: English is stupid anyway

MINNIE: Hey!

DOVE: Where the fuck have you been

MINNIE: Hey, so yeah, can I just get like, everyone gathered here for a minute?

(They're all gathered.)

MINNIE: Okay, cool.
So.
Uh.
We've been doing great work!

MAXX: Yeah.

MINNIE: And like.
The thing about new plays is that they like.
They're always changing and –

(Everyone groans.)

DOVE: Again?!

MAXX: But we already memorized all this shit!

JENNY: And we go up in like two weeks!

MINNIE: Sure yeah, and I get that.
　But, the thing is.
　Sister Ignatius has requested that I write a.
　Another scene, just expanding on what's already there –
　That's what she said – it's just expanding on what's already there –
　So.
　I'll be working on that.
　To expand.
　What's already there.
　But in the meantime, we're gonna still go with what we got!
　Everyone's doing great work and.
　I just.
　Thank you, all for like.
　Doing this.

IMOGENE: Thanks for having us.

(There's an odd moment between the two of them.)

MINNIE: All right, so let's just.
　Run it from the top.

*(The girls get into places.
DOVE walks over to her sister.)*

DOVE: What's up?

MINNIE: What, nothing –

DOVE: You're acting weird

MINNIE: I'm not acting nothing –

DOVE: Yes, you're doing that thing you do when you're nervous –

MINNIE: I don't do a thing –

DOVE: Tugging your earlobe –

(Minnie is tugging her earlobe. She catches herself. Stops.)

DOVE: You don't have to be so nervous. Shit's going good.

MINNIE: It's not that –

DOVE: Then what is it?

(Minnie says nothing. Dove puts her hand on Minnie's shoulder.)

DOVE: You can tell me you know.

(There's a moment between the two of them.)

MINNIE: Seriously, it's nothing it's just – Sister said if I don't write and put this new scene in the play, She's not gonna be able to let me pass and if I don't pass, I don't graduate and –

DOVE: I mean, what kinda scene is it?

(Minnie almost says something but. She doesn't.)

MINNIE: It doesn't matter - Are all the props set and everything?

DOVE: Yeah –

MINNIE: All right, doing a run in ten, all!

DOVE: Minnie -

MINNIE: Places, everyone. Places.

(Dove watches her sister walk away as – the scene transitions and we enter into -)

SCENE II

(The auditorium.
It's been kinda dolled up for mass.
There was a mass earlier in the day and it hasn't completely been converted back.
Specifically, there's a kneeler in the front, next to the stage, and a decent sized crucifix present.
Mathilda enters the space.
Notices the kneeler.
Hesitates but walks towards it.
Crosses herself and kneels.
Begins to pray.
Or at least she tries to, anyway.)

MATHILDA: It's.
　Kinda hard to do this not in a real church.
　I mean, I know You're everywhere and it shouldn't matter if I'm talking to you in a church or a bathroom –
　not that I would ever, ever talk to you in a bathroom –
　but, I dunno.
　It's hard to remember that You're here, sometimes.
　I used to feel you with me, all the time.
　In every breath, in every beat my heart makes, I could feel you.
　You were a part of my life, but now?
　I don't know what happened.
　Can you hear me, though?

(Maxx enters, her stockings are torn at the knees and her knees are a little bloody.
She sees Mathilda and stops in her tracks.)

MAXX: Oh, shit.

MATHILDA: Are you okay??

MAXX: Yeah, no, I'm fine
　I didn't think anybody'd be here.

MATHILDA: You're bleeding

MAXX: Yeah, I know
　Better look away, we all know how much you love blood –

MATHILDA: I didn't faint because of the blood –
You know what, never mind.
Go bleed all over the stage, see if I care.

(She starts to leave.)

MAXX: You should.
Wait.

MATHILDA: Oh yeah, so you make fun of me –

MAXX: 'Til the St. Tim boys go.
A bunch of them are out there.

MATHILDA: Oh.

MAXX: Yeah.

(Mathilda looks. Makes an aggressive, annoyed face.)

MATHILDA: They look so stupid out there

MAXX: Yeah, real dumb.

(Mathilda looks at Maxx. Takes pity on her.)

MATHILDA: You want a bandaid or something?

MAXX: You've got?

MATHILDA: Yup.

MAXX: You don't have to –

MATHILDA: It's okay

(She goes over to her. She takes out a mini first aid kit.)

MAXX: You carry around a first AID kit with you?

MATHILDA: It's just travel size.

(She takes the band aid out. Also takes out some disinfectant wipes.)

MAXX: Wow you're like.
   Really prepared for an injury

MATHILDA: Well, you never know.

MAXX: What are you, a girl scout or something

MATHILDA: Oh, I was.
   But we did mostly arts and crafts and sold cookies in girl scouts, boy scouts are the ones who're always supposed to be prepared or whatever

MAXX: This is like. Madd prepared.

MATHILDA: Sure.

MAXX: You wear long sleeves a lot.

MATHILDA: It's cold

MAXX: Is it?

(Mathilda doesn't respond.)

MAXX: I get it, you know.
   Takes one to know one.

(A quiet moment of recognition between the two of them. Mathilda breaks it, continues treating Maxx's cuts.)

MATHILDA: Are you going to tell me how this happened?

MAXX: It's not important.

MATHILDA: They're pretty bloody.

MAXX: It was stupid.

(Maxx hesitates but decides to tell her.)

MAXX: I was on my way to the bus but I wanted to stop at Buddy's first, to get a Pepsi and a Twix – I really wanted a Twix

MATHILDA: Oh yeah, Twix are really great

MAXX: Right? And so I was trying to get to Buddy's but there was like a crowd of St. Timothy guys blocking the way. And there's this guy, William DeFranco? you know him?

MATHILDA: I don't think so -

MAXX: he's like, super tall and kinda big but not fat and has dark curly hair and his mouth always kinda hangs open

MATHILDA: Oh yeah, I've seen him

MAXX: Yeah, him.
So like.
We been IM-ing lately?
Usually a night.
Like, late at night, when nobody else is on, we're both on and we been talking, usually just about anime – we both been watching Gundam, you know it?

MATHILDA: No

MAXX: Oh, it's good, it's madd good, you should watch it

MATHILDA: Okay

MAXX: it's on during Toonami

MATHILDA: right

MAXX: and so we're usually the only ones up and so we been talking the other day he kinda…
sent me a picture of his dick.

MATHILDA: What?

MAXX: Yeah, I guess he got a digital camera for his birthday so he took a picture of his dick and put it in an e-mail and didn't tell me what it was – like I didn't know I'd be opening a picture of his stupid dick when he sent it – and I opened it and it was there and I didn't know what to do so I just signed off and watched Gundam by myself

MATHILDA: That's so gross

MAXX: I know, right?
I mean, I've seen dicks before

MATHILDA: Oh yeah, who hasn't

MAXX: I've seen loads of dicks

MATHILDA: Totally

MAXX: But it was just.
Weird.
And so I've kinda been avoiding him, you know, like putting up an away message and shit, and he was out there today and – I dunno, we never really talked in real life, mostly just online so I was just walking by and he shouted out
YO MAXX, when're we hanging out?
And I was like I dunno and kept walking
and he was like
Bus is that way
And I was like
I know
And kept walking
and then he was suddenly
there?
Like, right in front of me, smiling and
he's got a real nice smile and
he was just standing there, smiling at me and I couldn't get past him so I started to feel like there was fire starting from inside'a me, burning my ears, behind my ears and I was saying Let me get past, William and he kept side stepping so I couldn't get past and he was smiling at me.
And he smelled like cologne
and his friends were standing there, laughing,

and he goes
Hey you got my e-mail?
and I was like, Yeah.
and he goes
You never told me what you thought of it
so I said something like, I dunno –
Yeah, that's because I was confused, I didn't know why you was sending me a picture of a peanut for and all his friends went like
OOOO, she got you!
And he was like
You know that's not true
So I said Yeah, you're right, it was more like a cashew and all his friends was laughing and calling him Peanut and shit and so I started walking away but then there were hands on my back and before I knew what was happening, the ground ate my knees and his friends were pulling him away and everyone else was just.
Staring at me.
So I.
Came here.

(Mathilda is done bandaging Maxx's knees.
They sit together, quiet.)

MAXX: Hey, I'm sorry for the other day

MATHILDA: It's fine

MAXX: I was being shitty

MATHILDA: Yeah, you were

MAXX: Why'd you faint?
  If it wasn't because of the blood

MATHILDA: You'll make fun of me

MAXX: I won't, I promise

MATHILDA: Like I can believe that

MAXX: You totally can

MATHILDA: Sure

(A beat.
She blurts it out:)

MATHILDA: I didn't know about the third hole

MAXX: What?

MATHILDA: I didn't know.
That.
We have three holes.
I thought there was only two.

MAXX: Oh

MATHILDA: And that the blood came from the same one we pee with and I didn't know that there was three and that one pees one bleeds and one poops and it messed me up and I couldn't even listen to what she was saying and my head starting feeling hot and cloudy and I tried to leave and I couldn't make it out in time so I fainted in front of everyone. Didn't even know she was talking about blood, just.
Whatever.

(There's a long pause.)

MAXX: I actually.
Thought the same thing before I found out

MATHILDA: You did?

MAXX: Yeah.

MATHILDA: Oh.
That actually.
Makes me feel better.

(A nice moment between them as we transition to –)

MOVEMENT III

(A passage of time movement –

we see the girls practicing the same scenes over and over, all directed by Minnie, just vignettes

we don't hear what they're saying but we get that they're starting to nail the play, they're doing it!!!

and in between takes,

we see Jenny and Imogene sneaking off and being v cute together

and Dove, Maxx and Mathilda getting closer and closer in between scenes

but we see Minnie kind of by herself, just watching, just directing the play, not really getting to be a part of the group, just watching the play come to life but not really taking part

The movement culminates in -)

SCENE III

(In a bathroom.
Maxx and Dove are standing outside a stall.
Mathilda is in the stall – we can see her feet.)

MAXX: Okay so the first you're gonna wanna do is relax

DOVE: Yeah, just relax

MATHILDA: Okay

MAXX: Just like.
  Don't think about it

DOVE: Yeah because if you think about it? You're gonna clench and you don't wanna clench, you wanna do the opposite of that

MAXX: Release, you're gonna wanna release

DOVE: Yeah, release!

MAXX AND DOVE: Release!

(There's a beat. They both listen intently.)

DOVE: You okay?

MATHILDA: I am
totally relaxed

MAXX and DOVE: Sure

MATHILDA: No, for real, I'm totally relaxed

DOVE: Just keep breathing through it

MATHILDA: Right

MAXX: Okay so now you're gonna wanna just
take off your underwear

DOVE: Yeah, like fully, because you're gonna have to spread
your legs

MATHILDA: Okay, got it.
Don't look.

(We see her underwear drop to the floor.)

DOVE: Okay, good

MATHILDA: You're looking!

MAXX: We're not *looking* looking

MATHILDA: Don't look!

DOVE: Okay, okay, we're not!
(they are)
Are you ready?

MATHILDA: Yeah.

MAXX: So okay, now you're gonna wanna spread your legs apart

DOVE : Yeah and like,
what I like to do is,
I put one leg up on the toilet and keep the other one on the ground

MAXX: Yeah, that's a good tip,
That's a pro tip, Mathilda, okay?

(We see Mathilda's leg go up.)

MATHILDA: Okay

MAXX: You feel balanced?

DOVE: It's important you feel balanced

MATHILDA: Yeah, yeah, no, yeah I feel totally, totally balanced

MAXX: Okay
good
okay
(Thinking about what the next logical step would be.)
okay
so
then
what you're gonna wanna do
is
Unwrap it

DOVE: Jesus, Maxx

MAXX: Hey, listen, I told Mathilda that I'd go step by fucking step and this is part of the steps

(We hear the crinkling of a tampon being unwrapped and see the paper drop to the floor.)

MATHILDA: I should pick that up

MAXX: You can get it later, keep your legs spread!

(Jenny enters, sees them and hears that last line, gives them all a look and just leaves.)

MATHILDA: Who was that?

MAXX: Sister Ignatius

MATHILDA: WHAT

DOVE: She's just fucking with you, keep your legs spread!

MAXX: Okay so you got the thing outta the wrapping?

DOVE: I'm pretty sure it's called an applicator

MAXX: Does it matter?!

MATHILDA: It is called an applicator!

MAXX: Okay, great, fine, so you got the applicator out?

MATHILDA: Yup!

MAXX: Okay so you see how there's like a part that it looks like you can push up?

MATHILDA: Yeah

MAXX: You're NOT gonna push it up by that, you're gonna grip it from the part right before it and then you push THAT part up INTO you before you push the other part up.

(There's a long silence.)

MATHILDA: What?

(Maxx pulls out a tampon and puts it under the stall, indicating what the fuck she's talking about.)

MAXX: See that?

MATHILDA: Okay, yeah!

MAXX: Okay so you're gonna wanna slowly push that part up

MATHILDA: Okay

MAXX: like, inside of you

MATHILDA: Okay

DOVE: and you have to relax

MATHILDA: Okay.

MAXX: yeah, just relax and push

(There's a long silence.)

MATHILDA: It won't go in!

MAXX: That's because you're stressed out, don't be stressed!

DOVE: Yeah just like BREATHE!

MATHILDA: I dunno how, how am I supposed to breathe?!

MAXX: You know, it's like uhh

DOVE: Just like

(Dove starts to do some deep breathing.
Gives Maxx a look like Come on, do these stupid breathing things with me.
They breathe together.
It gets relaxing.
They realize they haven't heard from Mathilda.
Direct their energy towards the stall door.
Wait.)

MATHILDA: Oh my god I did it
   I did it, it's up there!

MAXX: OKAY GREAT, NOW PUSH IT UP!

DOVE: But not too fast!

MAXX: It doesn't matter!

DOVE: It definitely does!

*(We see Mathilda's leg go down, off the seat.
Her underwear go up.
She opens the stall door.
Steps outside.)*

MATHILDA: I did it!

*(They all do a celebratory hug dance thing.
It's super joyful and awesome and wonderful.)*

SCENE IV

*(The auditorium.
There are decorations all around. Like real basic, streamers and stuff.
Minnie is standing in the middle of them, looking. She feels nostalgic in spite of herself.
Dove enters.)*

DOVE: Hey, sorry I'm late –

MINNIE: Had to cancel rehearsal today. Forgot, the gym's being used

DOVE: Yeah, what's all this corny shit for

MINNIE: The Father Daughter dance

DOVE: Oh.
  That.

MINNIE: Yeah.

DOVE: I forgot about that.

MINNIE: It's stupid.

DOVE: Yeah.

(There's a moment of quiet between the two of them.)

DOVE: You got to go with him.
  Twice.

MINNIE: Kinda.

DOVE: No, you did.
  I remember.
  I remember him coming out the bathroom in a suit and shit and he looked mad good and you two went off to the dance.

MINNIE: Yeah that was my Freshman year.
  Didn't go Sophomore year.

DOVE: What?

MINNIE: Yeah.
  I kinda.
  Pretended like I had a stomachache

DOVE: Why?

MINNIE: I just didn't wanna go.
  I dunno.
  I don't remember why.
  We had fun.
  The first time?
  Like, the first year, we had so much fun.
  Like, he had SO much fun.
  He danced with people who weren't even his daughters.
  And had me introducing him to everyone I could.
  And he was making small talk and dancing and taking pictures, too.
  He took a ton of pictures.
  When we got them developed he kept going And who's that? And who's that? Because a buncha them weren't even my friends or like even people I knew but he was just.
  So happy. And excited to be there.
  But then Sophomore year came around and I just.
  Didn't wanna go.

I told him I didn't feel good and he got me ginger ale and crackers,
He was already wearing his suit.
We'll go next year, he said and.

(Dove holds Minnie's hand.)

MINNIE: He was excited that we were all gonna go together.
Like, you me and him.
When you were a Freshman.
He said the summer before.
"You think we'll all go to the Father Daughter dance this year?"
And his face was just.
Lit up and hopeful and.
I was kinda excited about it, too.

DOVE: I'm sorry, Minnie.

(Minnie takes her hand away from Dove.)

MINNIE: Well, fuck it.
You don't have to be.
It's whatever, it's stupid and like.
Crying won't bring him back.

DOVE: Yeah, neither will your play.

(Minnie stops.)

MINNIE: I dunno what you're talking about.

DOVE: Yo, I know that you been wrapping him up in metaphors and shit and that nobody else
knows how much of you is true and is your shit

MINNIE: Dammit, Dove, this is why I told Mommy I didn't want you in this stupid play –

DOVE: What do you think she's gonna say when she sees it –

MINNIE: She better not come to see it

DOVE: Uh, I'm IN it, she BETTER come see it

MINNIE: Shut up, Dove, okay?!
   I'm serious, there's nothing.
   This shit's about nothing.
   It's not about Daddy.
   Or about me.
   It's not about anything it's just.
   Not important.

(She leaves. Dove is alone.)

SCENE V

(Sister Ignatius' office. She's sitting at her desk, grading papers. Mathilda knocks on the door, sticks her head in.)

MATHILDA: Hi – Is this, uh...still a good time?

SISTER IGNATIUS: Mathilda!
   Yes, yes of course.
   Come on in, please take a seat.

MATHILDA: Thank you, Sister. *(As she takes a seat)* Is everything – is everything okay or - ?

SISTER IGNATIUS: Oh, yes, of course!
   I just like to set up these meetings with as many Freshmen as I can.
   You know, a little Getting to know you as we embark on our four-year journey together.

MATHILDA: Oh, okay.
   Okay, cool!
   That's cool.

SISTER INGATIUS: I should have done this back in September but, you know how things go –

MATHILDA: Oh yeah, they get busy.

SISTER IGNATIUS: They do.
   So, Mathilda.
   How are you finding things?

MATHILDA: Oh, great. They're all great.

SISTER INGATIUS: Good!

MATHILDA: Our Lady of Sorrows is such a.
Great school.
And this is actually.
This is my first time in Catholic School!
And I.
Love it – I like it a lot.
I'd only been in public school before but, you know, used to go to religious education until I was confirmed last year and when we were deciding where to send me, my mom thought it would be best if she enrolled me in Catholic School for my high school education and I thought that sounded like a good idea because, uh, well, I'm actually, kinda thinking about becoming a nun later, in a few years, when I'm older and I thought that it would be really cool to, you know, have religion and mass and…all that. Stuff.

SISTER IGNATIUS: That's wonderful, Mathilda.

MATHILDA: Yeah.
I mean, I was thinking about it, I don't know.
Not yet.
I mean, I had started thinking about it like, last year.
Just, being involved in Church, it felt right,
but also like I should be doing more.
It's.
Hard to put into words, but.
Sometimes I feel it.
Inside of me, reverberating deep inside of me.

SISTER IGNATIUS: That so lovely to hear.
And I see here that you've gotten involved with the school play.

MATHILDA: Yeah.
And that's been great, too.
Like, maybe I want to be an actor.

SISTER IGNATIUS: An actor.

MATHILDA: Yeah, instead of a nun or -
Oh, I dunno, I'm just blathering.
I guess maybe it's all right that I don't have all the answers right now.
Right?

(beat)

SISTER IGNATIUS: You know what's funny.
Is I always wanted to be a priest when I was a child.
That's what I thought I wanted to do.
I used to tell my mother that and she'd laugh and tell me I couldn't
but I always wanted to.

MATHILDA: I bet you'd give a great homily.

SISTER IGNATIUS: Thank you, Mathilda. That's very kind.

MATHILDA: It's true though. I mean it.

SISTER IGNATIUS: Thank you.
But it's okay.
It truly, it's okay.
The rules are there because there are things larger than us at stake.
You know, I used to think I could change things so that I could be.
So that I could be a priest.
When I was your age, actually.
I grew up here, off Myrtle avenue and went to St. Barbara's every Sunday.
And one day, when I was fifteen, I just, marched in there, crossed the alter to the back, found Father Bernard and said
I want a meeting with the Bishop.
As though the Bishop could change anything, but what did I know, I was just a girl.
I need to see the Bishop!
And I wouldn't leave.
I just stood there, waiting for him to figure out a way to get me to see the Bishop.
He actually.
He promised me that I could see the Bishop but he also just

explained to me why.
It wasn't possible.
That the rules are there for us all to be safe.
To fit safely inside.
And sometimes, that's God.
Learning how to take our dreams out of our hearts and place them down.
To walk away from them.
To find that peace.
That's God, too.
(There's a moment of quiet)
Women, we can't be priests because it's not our role to play. It's the wrong thing to do, even though I wanted it to be right.

MATHILDA: But maybe. Maybe one day you could be –

SISTER IGNATIUS: No, and I wouldn't want to because it's wrong.
It would be wrong of me to do that and it was wrong of me to demand the Bishop.
It was wrong of me to desire it.
We know what's wrong and what's right.
It's a gift!
We know what's right.
And what's wrong.
And we have to hold onto what we know is right.
(beat)
Remember, Mathilda.
My door is always open.

(Mathilda nods. She leaves.)

SCENE VI

(The auditorium.
It's late at night – play rehearsal has been dragging on.
All the girls are there except for Minnie; Dove and Maxx are listening to each other's music, Mathilda is doing her homework, Jenny and Imogene are sitting, Jenny's head in Imogene's lap. There's a moment of quiet before we begin.)

JENNY: So…You wanna do our scene again or something?

IMOGENE: We already did it like twenty times, how many more times do we have to do it?

MATHILDA: We really need a director

DOVE: Minnie's director

MATHILDA: No, I mean separate from the playwright. *(mumbling)*
Justwouldbeamoreffectiveuseofourtimeisall

MAXX: Can't believe this is how I'm spending my Friday night at a PLAY REHEARSAL
how fucking lame.

DOVE: Yeah, okay, and what big fucking plans would you be doing if you weren't here

MAXX: This.
But at home.

MATHILDA: So this is better

(Maxx sticks her tongue out at Mathilda and she sticks it out back and they smile. It's nice.)

IMOGENE: Yo, Dove.

DOVE: What.

IMOGENE: How much longer do you think she's gonna be?

DOVE: I dunno, I'm just her sister.
She doesn't tell me anything.
You're her friend.

IMOGENE: Yeah, I guess.

JENNY: Oh shit, it's already almost eight.

DOVE: Seriously?

MAXX: Fuck

MATHILDA: How'd it get so late so fast?

DOVE: I dunno.

MAXX: Why can't school go by this fast?

DOVE: Right?

JENNY: I dunno.

MAXX: Well. Since we're all stuck here…

(She takes out a water bottle with dark liquid and shakes it a little.)

MATHILDA: What's that, iced tea?

MAXX: Whiskey and Gatorade

MATHILDA: Whiskey?!

JENNY: And GATORADE?

DOVE: Honest to god?

MAXX: Yeah

IMOGENE: What flavor Gatorade?

MAXX: Cherry. You want some?

IMOGENE: Sure.

(Imogene takes a swig from the waterbottle. Dove holds her hand out for it. She takes a swig, too. Imogene, too. Imogene holds the bottle out to Mathilda.)

MATHILDA: That's okay

MAXX: Aw, come on

DOVE: Yeah, it's just like drinking communion wine

MATHILDA: I don't think that's true

MAXX: Won't know unless you try it –

IMOGENE: Yeah, come on, just take a sip.

(Mathilda takes the bottle. Hesitates but takes a sip. Chikes a little but gets it down. Hands it back to Maxx.)

MAXX: Shit, I can't believe you did it!

MATHILDA: Yeah, well, I did. I totally, totally did.

DOVE: All right.

(Maxx passes the bottle around again and they all take another drink. Mathilda takes a larger sip than she did last time.)

MAXX: Yo.
  If you could like.
  Fuck.
  Anyone in the entire world,
  who would you fuck?

MATHILDA: Shane West!

MAXX: Really?

MATHILDA: I mean, I dunno.
  No, I mean, Yeah.
  YEAH!
  Yeah, I totally would lose my virginity to Shane West, I totallytotally would, he's just like really, he's really, he's just like, totally and completely
  Amazing

DOVE: He's all right

MATHILDA: Like, have you ever seen A Walk to Remember?

JENNY: Oh my god, it's so sad

MATHILDA: I know!!
   Like, if Shane West ever loved me?
   I would literally find out a way not to die

JENNY: I know, right

IMOGENE: OH and you know who's really hot?
   Michelle Rodriguez

MAXX: I love her

DOVE: OH! Usher!

MAXX: Fucking love Usher, holy shit –

JENNY: Nahnahnahnah wait, I got it, I got it - J. Lo.

IMOGENE: You're like obsessed with her

JENNY: Yeah, have you seen her?!

MATHILDA: She's ok

DOVE: Yo, it don't fuck with your hetero-ness to like admit someone who's hot is hot

MATHILDA: I just hate that song, the Jenny from the block song

JENNY: WHAT?

MATHILDA: It's just.
   On like.
   All the time.
   Every time you turn on the radio, it's on

JENNY: That ain't true

MATHILDA: I bet if I turn on the radio right now, it'll be on

IMOGENE: How much you wanna bet?

MATHILDA: Five. Full. Dollars.

IMOGENE: You're on.

(Mathilda fucks with the boombox. There's static, static, static. Maybe we hear a couple of other snips from popular songs of that era as she searches around.)

JENNY: See? I told you, it's not on all the time –

(Jenny from the Block starts to play.)

MATHILDA: See?!

JENNY: Oh my god, I love this song, though

(She gets up and starts to dance to it. Some of the other girls start to dance, maybe if they don't dance, they kinda sing along. It's fun and silly and everyone's having a good time when Minnie enters. She watches them for a second but gets into serious mode, walks over to the boombox and turns it off.)

JENNY: Yo, what're you doing?

MINNIE: I finished the scene!

DOVE: Finally!

MINNIE: It took a minute printing, there was a jam with the - I got copies for all of you.

JENNY: Okay, great!

IMOGENE: Can't wait to read this fucking scene that's so important.

(They all take the scene.)

MINNIE: All right, let's read it out loud!
　　Yeah, so the Devil is taking Claudio around different parts of hell.

IMOGENE: Why?

MINNIE: Because it's.
All right, so remember, I had to like, submit the play to Sister Ignatius since it's gone through so many changes and she had some concerns and thought I could make it more relevant to our lessons and.
Listen, she basically told me I had to put this shit in the play if I wanted to pass and it's.
I mean, we're all just playing, right?
So like.
Let's.
Just.
Read the scene.

IMOGENE: All right. *(as Claudio)* And what sinners have we here?

JENNY: *(as the Devil)* These are those who have committed sins of the flesh.

MAXX: *(as herself)* Oh, come on.

IMOGENE: *(as Claudio)* Sins of the Flesh?

JENNY: *(as the Devil)* Yes, those whose minds were tinged with lust.

DOVE: Seriously? *(as herself, reading the lines)* And those who have committed the sin of
having sex out of the sacred sacrament of marriage?

MAXX: Guess I'll be heading down to hell then.

DOVE: Come on, Minnie, this shit is whack!

IMOGENE: *(reading)* And those who commit a crime against their gender.
Those who have relationships with the gender that is their own –
(to Minnie) The fuck, Minnie.

MINNIE: Okay, listen -

IMOGENE: You don't believe this shit, do you?

MATHILDA: It is a sin.

(There's a cold moment.)

IMOGENE: Oh.
　Is it.

MATHILDA: Yes, homosexuality is a sin.

IMOGENE: You see that, Minnie, it's a sin

MINNIE: That's not what I meant, Mathilda –

MATHILDA: But it is a sin – It's literally in the Bible

MAXX: Just because shit's in the Bible don't make it true –

MATHILDA: God created us in His image and He created Adam and Eve so they could bring
life into this world –

MAXX: You think that actually happened?

MATHILDA: What, of course it happened

MINNIE: That's like allegory –

MATHILDA: We know what's right and wrong and it's IN the Bible!

MAXX: And what about "losing your virginity to Shane West" -

MATHILDA: I shouldn't have said that!

MINNIE: And it's not a sin, I didn't mean -

MATHILDA: But you wrote this!

IMOGENE: Yeah, you wrote this!

MINNIE: But, I don't believe it though –

MATHILDA: No, you wrote this!
And just because you don't want things to be sins doesn't mean that they're not sins.

MAXX: Are you fucking serious, Mathilda, that's so fucked up

MATHILDA: Like, what's the point of having rules if they're all just going to be broken, if we
all just run around acting like none of them matter at all?
Get mad at me all you want for telling the truth, but that doesn't make it any less the
truth.

MAXX: Well fuck you, then.

(A beat where Mathilda gathers herself.)

MATHILDA: You know what, I don't think I should be doing this play anymore.
I don't think we're on the same page.
And if this is what you all think, I have no desire to be.

(She leaves.
There's silence for a moment before Imogene turns to Minnie.)

IMOGENE: I guess we're all sins then, right?
Just by being women if we're playing by the rules of the bible.

MINNIE: No -

IMOGENE: You wrote it

MINNIE: So? That doesn't mean – it's nothing, it's -

IMOGENE: That's exactly what it means, you wrote it!

MINNIE: I didn't have a choice!

IMOGENE: But this shit is yours!
These are your words!
How're you gonna write them if you don't believe them?

MINNIE: I'm just trying to graduate high school

IMOGENE: Good for you I'm just trying to figure out how to be me in a world that don't want
me to be like this.

MINNIE: Come on, Imogene, no, I don't mean -

IMOGENE: Yeah, well, this is what I think of your shitty play. *(She rips up the pages.)*
Fuck your shit.

(She walks out of the auditorium. Jenny picks up both their bags and follows her out.)

MINNIE: Come on, I didn't mean it

(Maxx takes her shit, leaves. Dove picks up her shit.)

MINNIE: Dove, come on

DOVE: That shit's fucked up, Minnie.

MINNIE: But –

DOVE: You shouldn't have wrote it. Simple as that.

(Dove leaves. Minnie is left all alone.)

SCENE VII

(A classroom. SISTER IGNATIUS – RELIGION & MORALITY *is written on the board. We finally get to see her in her element as she teaches.)*

SISTER IGNATIUS: *Measure for Measure* by William Shakespeare.
I know, it might seem odd for us to look at a play during our lessons on morality and religion, but you'll actually find that questions of morality are a common thread for dramatists to weave through their work.
Measure for Measure could not be *Measure for Measure* if it were not for the great ethical dilemma presented to Isabella.

Will she go against her morals in order to save her brother?
If she sleeps with Angelo, her brother's life will be saved.
He will live.
But if she sleeps with Angelo, though she may not die for a hundred years, she will be condemning her soul to an eternal life in hell.
What is the ethical decision?
What is right?
Shakespeare gives Isabella an out, of course, by bringing in a character which makes it so the decision is rendered moot –
But what should she choose?
The question is a large one, it is not an easy one – it is her brother, after all, her own blood – but is her eternal life not worth more than the life of another?
Even if it is her brother?
Which decision is most Right?
What is the right thing to do.

(The scene ends and we enter -)

SCENE VIII

(The lunchroom. Imogene and Jenny are sitting together. Maxx is in another area. Dove is at a different table. Minnie enters. Everyone has a moment of seeing her and giving her the cold shoulder. She bravely walks over to Dove. Sits down. Dove ignores her.)

MINNIE: It's cool that we got taco Tuesdays back, right? I mean, it's just nice to know that
we're guaranteed tacos at least one day of the week, right?

DOVE: Sure.

MINNIE: It's cool that there's like. All different kinds of meat.

DOVE: mmm.

MINNIE: And cheese, too.

(Dove doesn't respond.)

MINNIE: Dove. Come on –

DOVE: What, I brought a sandwich.

MINNIE: You're gonna ignore me, too?

DOVE: I'm busy

MINNIE: Doing what?

DOVE: My own shit.

MINNIE: I just…Can I just sit here with you?

DOVE: Oh, now you know me.

MINNIE: What're you talking about?

DOVE: You serious?
You've been ignoring me all year!

MINNIE: Yeah but –

DOVE: Just now that you got a pocket of the school mad at you, now you know me enough to
sit with me, like what, because we're sisters I'm supposed to know you?
Or like, not be mad at you?

MINNIE: You know I didn't mean it –

DOVE: Yeah, but then why'd you do it?
Why'd you write that scene?
Just because Sister Ignatius told you to, so what?
Why'd you do that, Minnie?

MINNIE: I dunno.
I dunno!
I thought.
I thought it was the right thing to do –

DOVE: How could you possibly think it was the right thing to do

MINNIE: Sister Ignatius just made it seem like

DOVE: Man, what would Daddy think
That's all I keep thinking is what would he think.
He'd be so disappointed in you.

MINNIE: Stop it, Dove

DOVE: He would be!
Man, I know I'm your sister but you know what?
I don't have to be your friend just because it's convenient now.
So leave me alone.

(Dove leaves. All the girls, one by one, they leave. The scene is fluid and transitions to -)

SCENE IX

(The cafeteria transforms around Minnie, becoming the auditorium chapel. But it's more auditorium now than religious chapel. The theatre that has become her chapel. She begins to try to pray.)

MINNIE: Our Father who art in Heaven.
Our Father.
Who, art in Heaven, hallowed.
Our Father I.
I really fucked up.
Shit.
I really fucked up.
I fucked it all up, God, shit.
I didn't mean to but I.
I don't even know why I did it and.
But fuck, I don't.
I don't know what to do
I don't know what to do
What do I do, what to do I
God, why can't you tell me what to do?!
What's the point of talking to you when I don't even know if you're there?!
What's the point of talking to you when I don't even wanna talk to you,
I don't even wanna talk to God,
I wanna talk to you, dad.

I wanna talk to you.
I wanna talk to YOU
And people say that you can hear me but
you're THERE, not HERE and
I just want you here.
Daddy, I didn't mean.
I didn't mean for all that shit to be the last thing you heard from me.
I hear it in my head everyday, over and over, the last thing I said to you before you left that day
But I don't hate you, I never hated you I
I love you
I love you, dad
and I don't even know -
I'm just always asking you for forgiveness and it's something I'm never gonna get.
And I don't even know if I deserve it.
.
You always told me to do the right thing but how do I do that when what I think is the right thing is what they're saying is the wrong thing?
But I think they're wrong.
I think they're wrong.
.
No.
I know they're wrong.
I know that this shit is wrong, that what they're saying is wrong,
I know that they're wrong.
Fuck it, I know that they're wrong.
And I did the wrong thing but I'm gonna make it right.
I'm gonna make it right.

(Minnie leaves and walks right into -)

MOVEMENT IV

(Minnie begins to rewrite her play.

She rewrites it and rewrites it and all the pages of her play are fanned out in front of her.
As she rewrites, the other girls come forward – Jenny, Dove, Maxx. They look at her plans, they see her. They nod, they agree.

Mathilda comes over and looks at the plans. She shakes her head no. She leaves.

It's okay – Minnie's going to move forward with her plans anyway.

Imogene approaches. Minnie shows her the play. She says she's sorry. There's a moment. Then, Imogene hugs Minnie.

They break the hug – there's work to do. The movement ends as we enter into -)

SCENE X

(It's opening night of the play! They're in the middle of it. Minnie is playing the Devil, Dove is playing Claudio. Maxx, Imogene and Jenny are sinners in hell.)

DOVE: *(as Claudio)* And, Devil, what sinners have we here?

MINNIE: *(as the Devil)* Well, Claudio, these are those who have committed sins of the flesh

DOVE: *(as Claudio)* Sins of the Flesh?

MINNIE: *(as the Devil)* Yes, those whose minds were tinged with lust.
And those who have had sex out of the sacred sacrament of marriage,
and those who commit a crime against their gender,
those who have relationships with the gender that is their own –

IMOGENE: I am not a sin.

DOVE: *(as Claudio)* What was that?

MINNIE: *(as the Devil)* Uhh, nothing, nothing, don't listen to them –

JENNY: I am not a sin.

DOVE: *(as Claudio)* And that?

MINNIE: *(as the Devil)* Nothing, don't listen to –

MAXX: I am not a sin

IMOGENE: I am not a sin

JENNY: I am not a sin!

DOVE: It sounds like they're saying something

MAXX: I am not a sin!

IMOGENE: I am NOT a sin!

JENNY: I am not a SIN!

MINNIE: Don't listen to them, they're sinners!

IMOGENE: I am not a sin

MAXX: I am not a sin

JENNY: I am not a sin!

DOVE: I am not a sin!

(They all grab chairs while chanting I am not a sin, I am not a sin!)

MINNIE: Oh, no, I feel my power as the Devil fading!
I feel my hell being destroyed!
I have no power
I have no power!

(The lights start to get brighter and brighter.)

MINNIE: I am powerless to stop this!

(The houselights go on. Sister Ignatius has been watching the play. She is livid.)

SISTER IGNATIUS: Minerva, stop it!

(The girls all look to Minnie. But she stands next to Imogene. Holds her hand. Each of the girls hold one another's hands. We keep our hearts in our hands and they hold one another's hearts.)

MINNIE: We are not a sin.

IMOGENE: I am not a sin

JENNY: I am not a sin

MAXX: I am not a sin

DOVE: I am not a sin

(Sister Ignatius is shouting, trying to get them to stop.)

MINNIE: I am not a sin.

IMOGENE: I am not a sin

JENNY: I am not a sin

MAXX: I am not a sin

DOVE: I am not a sin

ALL: I am not a sin,
   I AM NOT A SIN,
   **I AM NOT A SIN,
   I AM NOT A –**

(The lights go out.)

Blackout.)

End of play.

NOTES